*The Awakening Letters*

30, 4, 2007
to Jean 2013
for David

# The Awakening Letters

Edited by

## Cynthia Sandys

and

## Rosamond Lehmann

JERSEY
NEVILLE SPEARMAN

First published in Great Britain in 1978 by
Neville Spearman (Jersey) Limited
PO Box 75, Normandy House, St Helier, Jersey
Channel Islands

Distributed by Neville Spearman Limited
The Priory Gate, Friars Street, Sudbury, Suffolk

ISBN 0 85978 033 3


*Second Impression May 1983*

Printed in Great Britain by
Redwood Burn Limited, Trowbridge, Wiltshire
and bound by Pegasus Bookbinding, Melksham, Wiltshire

# Contents

|  |  | Page |
|---|---|---|
| Foreword |  | 7 |
| Introduction |  | 9 |
| *Part I* | Awakenings | 11 |
| *Part II* | Various letters from: | 35 |
|  | Arthur (Lord Sandys) *Cynthia's husband* |  |
|  | The Angel | 37 |
|  | The Night Makers | 39 |
|  | Shakespeare | 43 |
|  | Executioners' Island | 45 |
|  | Joe (Sir Alvary Gascoigne) *Cynthia's brother* |  |
|  | The Tycoon | 47 |
|  | Isle of Man Disaster | 51 |
|  | Patricia *Cynthia's daughter* |  |
|  | Pergamon and Aesculapius | 55 |
|  | Sally *Rosamond Lehmann's daughter* |  |
|  | Words of Power | 59 |
|  | Church workers and the Pre-Christian Ray | 61 |
|  | The Sheep | 62 |
|  | An Intellectual Friend's Awakening | 64 |
| *Part III* | The Glastonbury Scripts | 67 |
| *Part IV* | Father Andrew Glazewski | 81 |
| *Part V* | Letters from Joe | 97 |
| *Part VI* | Letters from Sir Ronald Fraser and from/about Lord Dowding | 173 |
| *Part VII* | Sally's last letter | 183 |
|  | *Envoi* | 189 |

# Foreword

These scripts have been selected by Cynthia Sandys and myself from an immense number received through her mental mediumship over the last thirty years. Readers familiar with the two booklets entitled *Letters from our Daughters* (published by the College of Psychic Studies) will already have been introduced to Patricia, Cynthia's daughter, and Sally, my own daughter. More of their letters appear in the present volume, as well as remarkable communications from other relatives and friends . . . some distinguished during their lives on earth, some less known, or not known at all. The bulk of the material, however, comes from Cynthia's brother Joe, Sir Alvary Gascoigne. His letters form what is surely a unique record of one man's post mortem adventures and experiences.

Cynthia's preparation for her work is utterly simple and unassuming. Having disposed of her many household chores, she sits quietly, her writing pad on her lap; and after a period of deep meditation, takes up a pen and starts rapidly to write. She gives the impression of intense yet effortless concentration while she takes down what her spiritual hearing is receiving. The words come in an uninterrupted, unpunctuated flow, making a kind of delicate calligraphic web upon the paper. As each page is covered, I take it from her – that is when I am privileged to be present – and wait until the 'power' runs out and she lays down her pen. Afterwards I read the whole letter through with her, copy it and punctuate it. Whatever small part I have been able to contribute, my debt to her remains immeasurable.

Rosamond Lehmann

# Introduction

Many people are asking the perennial question. . . . 'What happens when we die . . .? Do we cease to be the people we have been on earth . . .? Do we change . . .? Do we recognise our friends . . .? Do we remember our earth life . . . ? Do we want, or need to return to Earth?'

We have chosen letters, from widely differing personalities, hoping that the message they bring may awaken a sense of the continuity of life, when we can say with increasing confidence . . .

'IN MY END IS MY BEGINNING'

Cynthia Sandys

# Part I

*Awakenings*

Oh Ma, I do love this plane, you never told me how frightfully well one feels. It's wonderful to be bounding with energy, and able to jump straight off the ground, and stay there! It makes me feel quite heady.

I can't understand how our earth could have become so awful, and yet remained within the reach of these lovely rays.

I'm very vague about the difference between the God-Ray and the Christ-Ray, all I know is this glorious feeling of utter peace – which breaks through everything, even my aching need for Johnny – even that gives way, and I feel as though some warm exhilarating substance was being poured into my veins, and remaking the whole cell fabric of my body.

They call it the 'Presence'.

It's not in the least like the idea of Presence that I had connected with God, something awe-inspiring that would make you hold your breath in wonder, and feel smaller than nothing – here was something exactly the reverse.

It literally pours into you, making you want to laugh and be gay, something that nestles closer than oneself to oneself – closer even than Johnny* – and yet it seems to be Johnny, or that Johnny is part of *it*. There is a feeling of breathing the same Divinity. It's the breathing that connects *us*. When Johnny thinks of me, we breathe together and the connecting breath is *God* – in fact, everything is God, but somehow we have been allowed to forget. . . .

* Her husband.

It's a strange thing dying; of course your mother was one of my first visitors. She came into the hospital where I was trying to puzzle out how and why I'd got there. I never liked hospitals. I supposed that I must have become unconscious, and been taken there in that state. When I asked for my wife, the delightful young nurses became so vague I could have shaken them! Then G. came in to see me and I asked about my wife, but she became silent, until at last I said, 'Do tell me, has something awful happened to her? Is she – dead? 'No,' said G. taking both my hands, 'but *you* are.'

I nearly sprang out of bed, it was so ridiculous. There was I in a most comfortable bed, in a charming room, with the prettiest of nurses, and very good food! I looked at G. in amazement, but she only laughed and reminded me she had died several years before me. I felt quite angry and put out, almost disappointed. I knew that I hadn't got very much longer to live. But I always thought death would be something majestic, awe inspiring and tremendous – some soul-shattering moment that I should *never* forget – something that would quell all my earthly desires, and turn me into something wiser and better, with vision and understanding. But here was I, dead according to G. but absolutely unchanged, excepting that I had neither pain nor discomfort. Instead I slept with ease, my meals were a great source of interest, and instead of hating the idea of food, here was I with the appetite of a school boy, enjoying dainties such as I had never tasted before! I could hardly complain about the conditions that I found myself in, but all the same I felt that I had been tricked by death. I had not been allowed to see the majesty of passing. Well, one must accept one's disappointments, especially with someone so gay and lovely as your mother, who now insisted upon my going to sleep. With a promise to be with me when I awoke.

I began to feel insecure. Dare I go to sleep? Where should I wake up? 'Oh, just here,' said G. 'But if you don't believe me I shall have to try and bring some of your immediate family.' Ah! now that was a problem, *why* hadn't they come with G. . . .? She

14

explained that owing to all the work that you and she had done of this nature, she was now a trained receptionist, and able to welcome us in the early stages, and that oddly enough I should probably not have been able to see my own family owing to their having gone further into Spirit Life and having shed the lower body. So I took her advice, and feeling drowsy I turned over, and slept.

When I woke up again G. was there beside me. We talked for a little, and then she said, 'Wouldn't you like to get up?' At first I feared that the pain might return, but as G. was quite sure that that couldn't happen, I asked her to get my clothes from one of the nurses. 'Oh, that's not necessary,' G. answered, 'you just get up out of bed and you'll find your clothes will be on you quite all right.' 'But I must wash and shave and so on. . . .' 'Oh no, that just happens here,' she replied.

How terribly slovenly it sounded . . . shambling into clothes which you never even put on; however I was under orders, so I did as I was bid. I got out of bed – without help – and sure enough, there was I fully dressed, and in *my own clothes*! That was rather startling. My own clothes, worn here and there by me! G. laughed and said, 'That comes of making such friends with your clothes that they grow an etheric double, and come too.'

'Now come into the garden and if you want to wash we'll bathe in the lake.' – a thing I hadn't done for years, the very thought made me shiver. However, off we went, moving with great ease so long as G. held my arm. Once she let go and I lost my balance and began to fall, but I never reached the ground. I lay on the air, as if it were a sofa. It was a peculiar feeling, and all the time a queer lightness was coming over me. I felt the same only stronger, but my body seemed to be of different texture, and when I moved my limbs they were so light, they felt almost like paper. There was an unreality which would have been terrifying if it had not been so pleasant. By the time we reached the lake I was no longer questioning whether I might or might not wish to bathe. My body seemed so intensely different from the old one, that when we reached the shore I was quite ready to jump in clothes and all, with the certainty that my clothes would have the good sense to withdraw and await my return! And sure enough, I was as free as air when I touched the water; and the water was quite unlike

15

anything I'd ever experienced before. The moment I touched it, I ceased to be the heavy practical person which I had been for the last eighty odd years, and became for the time the most feather-headed immortal!

You've no idea what fun it is to be absolutely feather-headed, I know it sounds too heartless when I remembered M. and all whom I'd left behind. But they were so distant at that moment, while I was breaking the shell which bound me to earth, and freeing myself in order to regain the glorious son-ship with Divinity. . . .

Nothing in all the world can take from one the inspiring moment when every cell in one's body becomes flooded with *light*. That is the sensation. All weight and confusion, all darkness of mind and body literally melt away, when the parenthood of God is made manifest.

I may have been disappointed by the brevity of death, but the wonder and beauty of the resurrection is beyond all explaining. I ceased to be, and yet I became more completely myself – plus so much more.

\*      \*      \*

I am so glad you can write with me again. I've been doing the exercises we all do on coming over here. I don't find them difficult. I've been doing them with your family and my own, whom I can now see quite plainly, but they have almost ceased to use their voices in speech, all intercourse being telepathic, and I'm not in the least word perfect at that yet!

I find the colour-bath treatments the sheerest joy. I'd like to write a little about them, because M. could do them on her plane.

I was taken into a valley, where a whole chain of tiny lakes lay like a string of precious stones set in green velvet, which seemed to be something between grass and moss. The first we dived into was pale gold, it felt like dropping straight into a buttercup, and the

16

refreshment was instantaneous. I could swim in it, but very little physical effort was required.

After a few moments in the first lake we went on to the second which was blue, and felt more like bathing in the sea as I knew it, but with a very great difference of vibration. Here the tremendous energy evoked by the first lake was toned down and we were given a great sense of peace and restfulness: no sense of weariness, it was more that of power held in reserve. Only a very short time was allowed for my first immersion in the blue lake, and then we went on to the third which was almost peach coloured, pale pink moving and changing into gold and pale orange. This, I was told, was my first direct contact with the Christ power, and with an immense sense of awe I dived into this moving vibrating pool. Even while I was standing on the bank I felt my whole body relaxing and contracting rhythmically as though it were automatically trying to align itself with this far higher and most wonderful vibration. I went deeper, allowing the water to close over me and I experienced a further awakening of power and intention, I felt cleansed and invigorated, to which was added a quite unlimited joy of life.

I have been so busy 'feeling' that I have not yet found any words to express these sensations. I feel quite breathless with all that has happened and is happening to me, I can only say, 'How could we have lived and breathed without the constant knowledge of the presence of God?' Now the old life has passed away, as Christ foretold, but we never really grasped his meaning: 'Behold I make all things new. . . .'

*This letter is from my daughter Patricia who came in spirit to the Memorial Service of a Master of Fox Hounds who had not given much thought to 'what happened next'. He passed over suddenly with a heart attack.*

You called me yesterday to meet B.S. I was proud to be asked to meet that splendid looking person. I remember him at Point to Point meetings and at the Hunt Ball. Once seen, never forgotten.

I was delighted to be able to go up to him and say, 'I'm the eldest of the Sandys daughters, they've sent me to welcome you.' He just stared at me as though I was quite crackers, and then he said very slowly, 'One of the Sandys girls from Himbleton? I remember you and your sister – but what on earth are you doing here?'

'Well, I'm not exactly on earth, that's just the point.' I answered. But that didn't click.

He was watching the ceremony and the service. Suddenly he caught his name being mentioned. 'Just as though I wasn't here myself – never got any notice to attend this service,' I heard him mutter, 'Always went when they asked me; everyone looks very depressed. What's it all about?'

I was standing quite close to him, and whispered: 'I think you'll understand soon.'

'But, God bless my soul, why shouldn't I understand now? And why are we standing in the aisle? You'd better go and find your family, and I'll press in here.'

He did so, finding to his surprise that no one made way, or took any notice of him. He looked so worried that I came closer and whispered, 'Don't you see, its *your* Service, all planned for you. . . . You knew it wouldn't be very long before you came over to us, and now it's happened, and they are all wishing you God Speed.'

He accepted it quite simply, and in the most practical voice he turned to me and said, 'Am I dead . . .? It seems an odd thing to ask a girl, but you seem to know what it's all about.' So I agreed, and urged him to go with me right up to the altar, and stand quite close to the Bishop. When the Blessing was given, such a draught of spirit power was invoked that we escaped straight through the roof on to another plane of living.

What a bright mind he has. I am leaving him now with a mass of old friends and relations. Some people who'd been killed in the First World War. One is very close, is he a brother? He was delighted to see them, and is now feeling very drowsy, and cut off from any sense of family loss. He will now probably sleep for some time, and so I have left him.

*This letter is from a very clever woman who 'died' suddenly from heart failure.*

I am amazed by all that has happened to me, I don't know where to begin. I do want you to know that Patricia has been the very hinge of my new understanding. She is so calm and unchanged, I simply couldn't believe it was she, and that both she and I had passed through death, and appeared to each other to be quite unchanged!

You've no idea what a help she was to me, with her quick wit and clear explanations. If only I could share all this with H. Do you think it would be possible? Patricia tells me that these separations are meant, so that we can learn to grow our perceptive powers without the use of form or sound. It's all enthrallingly interesting and full of possibilities. I had no idea that I should be wandering about the house and garden with my arm linked in H's. I seem to be quite unchanged. May I tell you how it all happened?

My heart gave out, and that was that. I fell into a coma, and woke up to find myself in a curious light. It wasn't sunlight or moonlight or electric light, it was different from any light I'd ever seen. I tried to go to sleep again but the light was rather disturbing, and to this were added voices, laughing and talking. I rather wished they'd stop. After all, I had been ill and they might remember, and leave me quiet. But the voices came nearer, and at last I could bear it no longer. I got up, but instead of feeling tired and ill, I was perfectly all right. At that moment someone waved to me, saying: 'It's lovely to see you awake at last.' I felt rather annoyed at not having been allowed to sleep on. Other people came pouring in from both sides, I half recognized some of them, and was on the point of saying so, when they vanished, and someone else took their place. Then suddenly I saw Pat, and I felt I must hold on to her. I said, 'Stay with me, I don't feel very well.' She sat down at once and explained just why I was feeling so muddled and insecure. It was a horrid feeling. I came over to this plane with no idea of what I should find. It was all half light, and half shadow. Patricia was an expert at explaining, and we were

20

soon in fits of laughter. I can't tell you how amusing she made it sound.

Then one of my own family whom I'd half recognized came back, and I suddenly grasped the fact that I'd died and left H. for ever. 'No *never* for *ever*,' said Pat, 'and if you like we'll go straight back to your home now!'

The very idea frightened me. What should I find? Would it be tolerable to see H. and the children? Pat was very practical. She said, 'I think you'd better get used to the idea first, and clear your mind of all this "death" business.' I longed to explain how hard it would be for H. to see it in this light, whereupon Pat, seeming to read by thoughts, replied, 'If he fails to make a mental contact, he'll have lost the opportunity which is one of the main objects of physical life.'

This was so completely new to me that I had to go away and think it over, and pray about it. I asked Pat about prayer, and she said, 'Oh it's wonderful here, just try.' – so we prayed together. How I wish I had the power to write and describe the wonderful release that came. God seemed to be within touch and breath. . . . I was enfolded by the Presence – it was beyond words. I felt that I had become immediately a part of the Divine Whole. I seemed to be a separate person and felt suddenly as though I'd been fitted into my place, like a piece in a jigsaw puzzle. If this is what death means – and if we die in order to bring this ecstasy into the lives of those we leave behind – I can only say how thankful I am that I have been allowed to pass over so easily, and to learn this without any further waste of time.

*[Received from the same writer one year later.]*

Pat has shown me how to 'get moving' as she calls it. I find so many people come over here quite unprepared, they are often completely shattered by the shock of discovering that they are dead. They have always avoided discussing or even thinking of it. Then it happens, and they drive themselves quite silly over the fact that their relations are unable to see or hear them, while they themselves are fully able to see the grief of those left behind. In this state they often refuse all help from us, and when they become

21

used to this unseen life they settle down to wait in comparative comfort. When their relations join them, they either continue to wait for someone else, or they begin to ask themselves, what else is there? And having done nothing on this side, they have built up a sort of 'waiting wall' which grows automatically between them and the next stage of life.

I've tried to wake up some of my old friends, and with Pat's help I've jolted some of them out of these ruts. It seems to me terribly important that *we* should evolve, and Pat and I are both doing this, so that when our beloveds join us we shall be able to help them.

*This letter is from a country Doctor, a General Practitioner.*

May I write? I was a doctor on earth, and I knew you all intimately, my name is Sykes. I was very fond of you all, but I had no use for religion or faith healing, or any of those sentimental emotions. Pain was far too real to be tackled like that. I suffered, and came over in a rather battered state of mind. There seemed to be so much useless suffering and unhappiness, and it seemed to be all without rhyme or reason. Then I woke up in a hospital. I had died at home and could not think how I'd got there. But it was a most wonderful place. I became instantly so much excited by what I saw and felt that I had no idea that I was looking at etheric treatment.

A doctor came over to me, and asked how I was feeling adding, 'We shall be glad to teach you all we know.' Well, I wasn't asking anything except in my own mind, but he was answering my unspoken thought. I found myself wondering if my blood pressure could be taken, and he replied at once, 'Yes, if you like, but we don't need to here, the blood circulates quite differently.' What did he mean . . .? He sat down beside me, and out of nowhere a diagram appeared showing the organs and arteries of my new body. 'This is what you've got to work on now,' he explained. I thought I must be going mad. Here was a diagram of a body, similar in shape to the one I knew, but with feeding ducts, digestive organs and so on, of a much simpler kind.

I noticed all the pressure points of the body were marked with 'light intake', 'colour intake', 'heat intake', and so on. The digestive organs seemed to be on a rotary system. It looked like one large fly-wheel that drew in from all sides the white and coloured rays, transforming them into energy and *life* such as I am now experiencing. After a few moments he sensed that I couldn't take in any more. The diagram vanished and I slept – thinking, thinking, thinking. . . .

The next thing that I remember was hearing music, lovely deep music like a church organ. I felt as though it were putting strength and weight into me. If I had felt lightheaded before, that had now gone. I was being *fed*, that was the sensation, definitely *fed on*

23

*music*, and when I became replete I slept again. . . .

May I write again some time?

*       *       *

Yes, I should like to go on. I told you that I came over here with no understanding or belief in the spiritual life. I did not deny that it existed, but it was so far disassociated from ordinary life as to be completely out of touch for the ordinary man and woman. Now I found it was *me* and people like me, who were deflecting the healing rays from reaching the earth. Of course I am most deeply ashamed, and I have taken great trouble and care to learn the way of passing it into your bodies. I know you all very well on both sides of the curtain of life, and I also know that you are often imploring aid for others, so I would like to work through you and your husband, if you will let me? Look upon me as the doctor whom you knew and explain the trouble to me in mind, and ask that the power which surrounds and interpenetrates us all may be focussed for the greater health of those whom you want to heal.

I would like to go on telling you about my experiences on first coming over here. I told you about the diagram of the etheric body, and how I took in all I could, and then I slept.

On waking, I found the same man beside me. He asked me at once if I would like to come into the operating theatre. I said yes, but I must dress first. Then I realized how strange it all was. The moment I got out of bed I *was* dressed! and feeling well and rested and eager to learn *anything*.

He took my arm to steady me as the ground seemed to rise and fall and I had no power of balancing in my new body. We floated out through the wall to my great amazement, and found ourselves in a garden with a lake surrounded by enormous trees. When we reached the edge of the lake he made as though he wanted to push me in, but I found instead that I was sliding above the lake without

24

touching the water, and fearing that the spell should break, and I should fall with a splash at any moment, I determined to accept it all as quite natural, and tried to think of the lake as not a watery lake at all, and soon I had many other things to think about. In the centre radiating outwards on all sides were beautiful coloured rays, flashing such bright colours that by the time we reached the centre I was feeling terribly giddy. The doctor sensing my discomfort said at once, 'Look down,' which I did, into a blue of such healing calm that the giddiness left me at once. Then he said, 'Look up,' and again I met this strange mesmeric blue, and felt myself sandwiched in between these two belts of blue with the flashing glowing rays all round me. I'd lost sight of the lake and the trees as such, but now I saw that people were coming and going among us, drawing others with them who seemed to be asleep or unconscious.

Many of these people had crippled twisted bodies. I saw the helpers lay them in a horizontal position on a ray, using it as though it were a table, straighten out their limbs quite simply, then focus another ray upon them and then, and still in a sleep state, float them away out of our sight. I was gasping with questions, and my doctor friend needed no further vocal word, but started off at once to explain.

These were mostly the etheric bodies of people who had suffered from polio, or been crippled or paralysed in some way. They had all to be treated before they woke up and it was all quite simple. He explained that there was no illness of the etheric body, they only became crumpled like a dress which is always being worn crooked. They have to be straightened and strengthened, and that is all.

I asked what would happen if we did that on earth? He said: 'It all depends on the patient. Here no one thwarts you in mind, while on the physical plane they are always searching for a physical explanation, but if the human mind could accept simple healing it would be healed.'

So my first treatment is, straighten your body when you go to bed so that the force can flow up and down without hindrance.

*　　*　　*

Thank you, I should like to go on. It's the most extraordinary thing, but I feel so much better, more myself, less vague and far more composed after I have been writing through you. It seems to focus my mind by giving me a sense of that rock-like existence, which it was on the physical plane.

I see now that I have lived a very narrow life with few new ideas, and it's a hard job breaking up the habits of seventy odd years. But we have to do it. No one makes us, but we have to become elastic in mind and body. I must tell you that I felt very cumbersome when we first started writing. It was so new to me. But I feel already that you are pushing me on, giving me an incentive to work through you on the physical plane where my heart and mind are still active.

I had no idea that this was possible, nor was it to this extent in my day, but now there are many, many doctors over here who are ready and anxious to work through you.

I was starved of opportunity, I never met the big men of my day, and I longed to be in the swim. Now I feel I am right there, and it's most intoxicating; that is why I said that writing with you makes me realize the constriction of earthly life again, and the feeling of inability to heal, which was so often my lot. Now I see no reason for any healing whatsoever to fail.

When you send us to anyone in need of healing, try and do so during the hours when they would normally be sleeping, then we have the ego out of gear as it were, with the clutch running freely. This time of sleep is most vital. Sleep corrects the whole set up of the mental machine. So when you prepare for sleep you cannot take too much trouble, either for yourself or for your patient. The quiet drift into sleep is the vital moment.

*This letter is about a woman who 'died' suddenly as a result of a road accident.*


*Patricia writes:*

You sent me out to find Mrs. W. I barely know her, but she came over very suddenly and it has been an awful shock. She had never really thought much about it. She couldn't make out where she was, and kept on asking for her dogs and her grandchildren and her husband, and how glad she'd be to see Richard. . . . I was rather nonplussed, but I promised to do what I could and tried to calm her. After a few minutes she yawned and said, 'Oh my God, I had such a bad night at the hospital I really must go to sleep. Why did they say I was all broken to bits? I'm not. I did feel rotten but that's all over now.' And so I left her sleeping.


*[Continued some days later.]*

W. is getting on very well. She was awake when I returned and I heard her laughing and saying, 'Can't you get me some cigarettes in this place?' She doesn't really know yet, as she isn't properly awake, but every moment she is growing more beautiful and vital and young. I've never seen anyone change so quickly. I think she must have been pinned down in some way on earth.

It's lovely having more people from Worcestershire, even though I didn't know her. She knew you, and when I told her my name she remembered at once and said, 'Oh, the Sandyses, yes, of course, I haven't seen them for ages, are they here?' I said, not exactly, but that I often saw you.

'But what are you doing?' was her next question. I replied that I worked in a hospital and did a lot of botany. I said that quite naturally, forgetting that they were great gardeners. But W. leapt at it, 'What do you do? Tell me about it,' then looking up she said, 'What are those flowers over there?'

'Poppies,' I told her, 'I'll fetch you some.' So I brought her an armful and she responded immediately: it was like putting two

27

beads of mercury together. W. seized them from me saying, 'Oh, these are wonderful, but they are roses.'

'No,' I persisted, 'Just scented poppies, and they will soon make you feel sleepy.'

'Yes, they have already. I must sleep now, but come back and talk to me about flowers. I love them, I can't live without them . . .' and then she slept.

*This letter is from a Church of Ireland Clergyman in a remote district of Western Ireland.*

I woke up after the sleep of death, not in a garden like many others, but in Bunbeg church during Celebration. I was in front of the altar. At first I thought I must have fainted, and tried to regain my place in the service. Then, I found that a stranger was officiating, and no one seemed to notice me, so I remained where I was. The Consecration took place and the priest partook of the bread and wine, and at that precise moment the east end of the church disappeared. . . . It was as though all the stones and mortar were nothing but a curtain which had been drawn aside in one moment, and in its place a rich light flamed its way into the church. It seemed as though it would burn the altar; it enveloped the priest in a pillar of fire, which lapped round each communicant in turn; and they went back to their pews with the scent and glow of God's flame upon them.

I was so dazzled and stupefied that I do not know exactly what I did, or if the flame came near to me, but suddenly the light faded and the church wall closed up again, and people filed out. I turned to the priest full of questions, but of course he could neither see nor hear me, and I was thinking how very rude he was, when an older priest stepped down from the sanctuary, whom I had not noticed seeing there before, and asked if he could explain anything to me. I gasped, and began reeling off questions, to which he made the most wonderful answers. The old priest said, 'Come and see a little more,' and before I knew what had happened we were walking over the air to the Islands. He held my hand tightly, or I should have fallen. In a few moments we were at the little church at Carrickfinn. I loved it, and had spent much time in prayer within its walls.

When we entered I saw a glow, almost a fiery glow round the altar. Seeing my surprise the priest paused and pointing to it he said, 'That is the result of your prayer, Williams.'

'But,' I said, 'how is it possible to *see* the results?'

'Because, you are now looking at the *causes* and *results*.' I couldn't think what he meant, was I dreaming? No, I was up and walking about in my usual clothes. But, the idea came suddenly. 'You are out of this plane forever. Now you will see *only* the outcome of your thoughts and actions.' I felt bewildered. Was I in a trance? 'No,' said the priest looking straight at me, 'You have served your time on earth and now you are a minister of Christ on the next plane.'

You can't think what that meant to me. I just couldn't believe it. I had been ill and in some pain, but to come over so easily, and to go on with my work in the same place was unbelievable. . . .

I have been told to tell you all this because in moments of disappointment or weariness you are apt to feel that the earthly failure and the heavenly one are the same; but the motive and desire, however wayward, reaches God, the merciful and understanding Father. This is what happened to me, a very faint follower after Christ.

*This letter was written by a young woman, a very talented writer, who died after a long and painful illness.*

You have been thinking about me so often lately that I've been able to come quite close, and now I can write through you! What fun. I should love to send messages home, but no one is ready to receive them. I should upset my family badly, if I started doing anything so reckless. But I should like one old friend to hear from me. She always knew that there was an immortality in words, so I can reach her through worlds of words. How we used to shut ourselves from the world and just enjoy the printed word. I go on with my words but they are a different type now and run more smoothly from my teeming brain than ever from my pen. Tell her – oh tell her that I'm *free* – thought carries me on an ever beyonding reach. We do not play hide and seek with our thoughts over here, but we ride them as though they were horses with tossing manes. Everything is attainable – you have to work for success, but there is no frustration. Can I tell you about my life?

I came over unhappily, not as the old who die easily, and fall like ripe seeds matured and ready for the soil of spirit life. I came through the dark valley – but oh, nothing in all my lives can touch the beauty of awakening. . . . In misery I lost myself in unconsciousness, but I awoke to a glory beyond the morning sun. . . . I had forgotten ecstasy, but it was waiting for me with a fullness of perception that breaks through fancy and escapes my pen – the feeling of absorption into the very Godhead itself is the only way I can describe it.

That is what happens to us who suffer: Christ in the fullness of his divine sympathy embraces and endows us with a power to merge, and literally to cease our individual consciousness within the radiance of his Being. One is enfolded within a consciousness so lovely, so profound, that I knew no loss of self, but I became just one more sentient part of the Christ consciousness, knowing and feeling only the greatness of love, and within that over-whelming ecstasy I hung poised between life and life, until the broken particles of the suffering me had grown together in this love solution. As the time grew near for me to become again just

31

Barbara, I found myself not less but more, far more than I had ever imagined possible.


*[Later]*

I was telling you how I woke up to find I had a light active body, no pain, nothing to worry about, it was *bliss*. I can't tell you how I felt. I had been shut away in pain and darkness, my illness had separated me from all healthy creatures until I felt a pariah. I knew that the time must come, and when it did it was like waking up after a nightmare. For a time I was so happy in just being alive and well, that I never missed anyone. I know that sounds unkind, and as though my love had gone with my physical body, but it wasn't that. I, Barbara, had died in spirit long ago, long before I left my physical body, so it was no shock to be parted from them all, but – I can say it to you – it was infinite *peace*. No more efforts to keep back my tears, no more agonizing planning for my children and no more having to face their disappointment when I ceased to play my part in the family. No, the cards had all been played and I was outside the game, and *so happy*. It was worth it all to have that wonderful feeling, that I had finished. . . .

I suppose I slipped in and out of consciousness, I remember feeling that it was like a perfect summer day in the most glorious country. I could see a lake and some mountains, and I distinctly felt that I was lying in the heather. I was alone. I've always loved being alone, and lately it became an obsession. I had no need to act. I *was* alone.

I must have slept from time to time, and when I had slept the weariness out of my bones I remember lying in complete harmony and comfort, waiting for the next event, and it came in the form of a voice. I couldn't see anyone. It was just a voice calling me by name. But my name sounded so beautiful, I hardly recognized it. I sat up in order to listen more easily. The voice seemed to be coming from everywhere, and it told me to get up and walk to the lake and bathe, and see how the water would give me back my strength. I got up without any effort, and we walked, the voice and I, towards the lake. When I got there it seemed only natural to jump in from an overhanging rock, and the moment I touched the

32

water I knew that I was experiencing *real* life for the first time. These were the waters of Lethe where one learns and forgets. . . . I found ecstasy in that lake. The power of movement and the sense of force within me were beyond anything I could ever imagine. How long the voice and I stayed in the water I have no idea. It might have been hours or days.

I found I could dive to immense depths, lie on the surface and rest without any special effort, and all the time the voice was with me, telling me, holding me, and urging me to do more and make new efforts, to look around and see the country, and then lastly to listen. . . . I lay and listened. At first I heard nothing but the lapping of the water, then a tiny network of sound emerged. It grew until I could define notes, and then gradually the whole orchestra of Heaven burst forth – and I just lay and listened.

# Part II

*Miscellaneous letters from communicators, which we have selected for their variety and, we hope, their exceptional interest*

*Four letters from Arthur, Lord Sandys (Cynthia's husband)*

## THE ANGEL

So you want to hear more about angels. This is a far call, even for us. I'm very much interested in angels, and on the fairly rare occasions when I've seen them, I've been fascinated by their grace and beauty.

They do not penetrate the lower etheric atmosphere excepting at Christmas, and I think Easter, to some extent. But Christmas is the feast of earth – Easter, that of heaven.

On the Eve of Christmas, angels can be seen almost everywhere in the holy places – Westminster Abbey, St Paul's, Iona, Glastonbury, and so on. My first encounter was in Westminster Abbey after visiting the Battle of Britain Chapel: there was a beautiful angel on guard at the door. I tried to communicate with his high spirit, but ordinary vibrations did not register. He, or she, was in deep meditation, so I slipped away, keeping an eye on the possibility of a change in the forces of his thought; but it went on, and the stillness of his figure looked as though he had been carved in stone.

I came back and tried to sense the vibrations, but they were completely different from ours, longer, and slower, altogether outside time as we know it. I waited, and after a long interval he sighed and moved, caught sight of me, and smiled, and then said: 'Earthman, you are no airman.' 'No,' I confessed, 'I am only an earth soldier.' He sighed again saying, 'I am nearer to the flying men, but I have been on Flanders fields too, and that is where you come from, I see now.' I was very surprised, time has taken me so far from those days; I did not expect the angel hosts to sense the mud of Flanders on my boots today.

But I was wrong. He shuddered, and continued: 'All this time, and you still carry horror in your aura.' I said, 'How can I free myself of these experiences?' The angel came quite close to me, and I seemed to be in the centre of a mighty rushing wind. When it had passed, the angel had vanished, but the sigh which I caught on the wind said, 'Now you are free.'

This made me realize that I had held on to the vibrations of France and Flanders, treasuring them, and holding them far too close for my advancement. Now I can move and think much faster in consequence; and I know that it is all due to the angel.

# THE NIGHT MAKERS

I am so grateful to you for keeping to the régime of prayer together at the same hour. It's very good for me to have a routine, that is something that we all miss over here, where there is no natural routine of night and day to set the tenor, or meal times, or seasons to set the mode of life, or to alter the endless sunshine and beauty of timeless perfection. Many people find this very irksome; some have longed so intensely to return to night and day that they have formed a little group called 'Night Makers'. They meet and induce darkness, relaxation and sleep. It all began from a desire to make a pause between 'doing' and 'being', and now it has grown into something mystical. They 'see' the night as we used to in clear weather, with the moon and stars, and become conscious of the subjective influence of reflected light. 'Moon-struck' we used to call it. But here, it is something quite tangible. The Moon-Rayers have quite a curiously different approach, and I, for one, am studying this most carefully. They are all ardent earth-workers, so they synchronize their nights with yours, in order to have more power and help during sleep. They are used by the healers and artists, and most of the groups of inspirational workers.

Pat let me find them all by myself, and it came about like this:

I was sitting in the garden of thought, trying to space out my life, which is hard at first, when timelessness lets the weeks through, while one is just thinking over one theme – interrupted now and then by your constant calls – which at first made my days; and though they seemed to come in an erratic pattern to you, to me they seemed fixed and regular. Your need for me rose whenever the substance of my last close contact was exhausted; this made a routine for me to work by. But it was not sufficient, and I found I was all awry with times and seasons on earth; and if I were to be really useful, I must align myself more clearly.

I was thinking this over, when a man whom I'd known in the Engineers, came up to me and asked if I knew about the Night Makers. I said, 'No, who are they?' and he explained, having seen the trend of my thoughts, that if I needed routine and a time-check in my life, I should join them. So he took me to one of these night areas. It was most exciting.

Gradually the sunshine ceased, and twilight, and then darkness fell, as we entered a cypress grove. The stars were brighter than I had ever seen them; and the moon, though not 'lamping San Miniato' was lamping this garden of beauty and stillness. It was an entirely new sensation of peace.

This night light which was being produced artificially, was specially for healing and inspiration during sleep. I watched and listened and gradually I saw how to use it.

My Royal Engineer friend drew in the vibrations at once and went off on his private line, leaving me standing in the cypress garden flooded with moonlight. People were coming and going; many were being brought in their sleep bodies for health and refreshment; others were guarding the lines of return against the entry of less evolved spirits. This sounds selective, which of course it is. One can only work upon the level of one's own vibration. But many who come over with a grudge against vested interest, or class feeling, are forever trying to push their way into the spheres nearest to earth which have been set up specially to help all of you in the body.

I wandered round the defences; according to my army training they were non-existent; but I soon found out that that was not so. Masses and masses of tiny threads of force had been spun like a spider's web all over the area, and anyone vibrating at a purely selfish level, with the desire to force their way in, reacted immediately in the central staff office. Then, instead of a curt refusal of entry, such as I might have given on duty, someone was sent at once to *help* the intruder. They were dealing with this when I arrived, and I asked if I could join the defence party, and watch how it was done.

I started off with my new friends, and we soon met the intruder, a big bully of a man, in the twilight area, and the scene went as follows:

The guard welcomed the newcomer with, 'Hello, are you searching for darkness, after all the dreariness of earth?'

'No,' was the answer. 'But I want to go everywhere, and I was told this was a closed area. I've come away from all that, and I want to go places. What's your answer?'

40

'Come and see for yourself.'

This staggered me. Then, unseen by the intruder, an envelope of non-seeing was spun into his aura, and we proceeded back to the garden. Gradually the dark clear moonlight replaced the twilight and the full beauty of the garden came into view. But the intruder saw only darkness within, and profound fear penetrated into his aura. He was lost in it. He put out a hand for guidance and finding that of the guard, he said, 'Isn't there any light?'

'Well no. That's the idea, don't you like it?'

'No, take me back at once into the sunshine.' So we did, leaving him a wiser, and perhaps, a humbler man.

I was glad to be able to spin out my days in this manner. When one comes over here with the strength to carry one through endless daytime, the element of time ceases, it flows on and on, like a moving carpet. It may feel like centuries to you since I left my body, but to me it feels like yesterday, in spite of all the newness and excitement of this life. Those who have studied meditation provoked this period of night which I was telling you about. They found as they produced night they gained an inner vision and another type of power which could only accumulate through the use of an unseen light, something which they called the inner sun. This was what I was searching for, and after seeing the ability of the novice to feel the sunlight as I told you in my last letter, I ceased to question the curious feeling that was surging up in me. There was a sense of tingling. A curious electrical charge seemed to be diffused all round me. I was told, 'This is what you must now use to enlarge the depth and colour of your aura, and the strength of its penetration.' I was delighted and set to work trying to breathe this intangible force into myself.

At first I could do nothing with it; then it suddenly took hold and I felt like a balloon that you used to blow up for the children. At first the sensation was exhilarating, but it soon became tense, and I felt as though my aura was cracking at every pore. I tried to let go and escape, but I couldn't. 'What happens now?' I asked, 'Go on, don't worry about the sense of expansion, that is unlimited. You still hold all these ideas of limitation. Throw off the sense of bursting and *go on*. . . .' All very well, but the sense of bursting was so strong, that I called on Pat to come and help me. She came, and *how* she laughed. I'd gone off on my own, and as usual, got

41

into trouble, as she put it! Exactly how she turned off the taps and got me back into daylight I can't remember. The next thing I knew, we were sitting on the grass laughing about it, and she was telling me that I'd gone too far and too fast, as usual. 'You're too precocious, Pa,' was her main comment.

This night life of mine is now becoming one of my sources of power. If you found me distant or difficult to contact, as you did yesterday, it's because I haven't quite grown up to the size of my aura. Just the reverse of being too big for one's boots!

Pat keeps on reminding me that there's not a dull minute over here, and I find this to be more and more true as I adventure out alone. Soon I shall go back to Ferguson, my old R.E. friend, and see what I can do to stir him. (His reply, when it was mentioned that the urge to go on is very great, had been, 'Oh, don't worry about that, if you take no notice of it, it goes off!')

Pat says, 'Don't worry people to develop if they've no wish to. It means their earth ties are too strong, and they had better rest and relax in the sunshine, and when they have exhausted that pleasure, they will either move on naturally or return to earth in another body.'

# SHAKESPEARE

I'm going to talk about our world, not yours. You need to think more, pray more, and feel more clearly the effect of our rays and influences.

First I am going to tell you about Shakespeare. It's four centuries since his birth, and so many people are thinking towards him, that he has returned to my plane, and we have all seen, heard, and enjoyed the billows of laughter, the riotous fun, and the calm incisive philosophy which accompanies him everywhere. As a personality, he is full of warmth and wit, completely in charge of his ego, a prince among men. How he makes me laugh! – far more than ever before, because I can now understand the Elizabethans' enormous pleasure in plain jokes. I am struck by the tremendous amount of good our comedians do. They relax the whole structure of the tense mental frame, and give us a common note of laughter.

My first meeting with Shakespeare was just as he was listening to the 'call' that went out for his anniversary at Stratford. I saw him trying to remember just how much, or how little Stratford meant to him. Stepping closer, I asked if he continued to write plays on the etheric, or whether he could influence the earth actors to see things as he saw them.

He looked at me for some moments, and then said, 'No, there is no need. The world has moved on, but the things I wrote aren't tied down to one period. I'm so glad human nature doesn't really change. It's still dishonest and lazy, honourable and exalted; all the things that are such fun to portray. Even now, the England which I loved is still set in a silver sea. She has grown, but the essentials are unchanged. The soldiers still grumble, the wives still quarrel, and attack each other and their husbands: mankind is still filled with curiosity, and tediously obstinate. Yes, in themselves they are just the same. I could live in modern England and enjoy it just as much, perhaps more so, because of these new exciting changes, which are neither so new, or so exciting to us, having used these faculties in the etheric to a far greater extent; but now, to see them ensconced on earth gives novel flavour. This wireless as you call it, with which you "see" in your homes that which is going on elsewhere – soon – if you only knew it, you could, and probably will see things projected from another planet. . . . Oh! they are watching you all, you precocious children! One day, you will see us projected on the screen of vision, and then how will you accept this prodigy of science? It will all fall within your scope of science-life and reasoning, and all the greatness will be robbed by the smallness of men's minds. . . . Will they never grow to match the universe in which we live?'

And then he turned away, and entered into one of his long silences. Watching humanity, and still caring for you all, that is what makes Shakespeare so great. He loves mankind, it's a Christ-like faculty, and because of that, he suffers and is reborn with almost every performance of his plays.

Shakespeare can never lose touch because you are all continually calling him; and his plays cannot lose the living touch, because he is re-enacting them through the minds of the actors and producers, all the time.

# THE EXECUTIONERS' ISLAND

When you were at the Hotel on the island, I saw and spoke to several wraiths, who were most unhappy and horrified. I discovered that they had been executioners and as their lives were sought by all the townsfolk, they went in fear of their lives; and after their lives – which all seem to have ended violently – they continued in this state.

I said; 'What are you afraid of?'

'Everything,' was the answer, 'Excepting you, you bring such a sense of calm.'

Rather pleased, I went on, 'Have you never left this island?'

'No. No. We can't leave it. If we do we shall be killed – horribly.'

'But you are already dead. You can't suffer bodily pain any more.'

They looked at me in astonishment, and said, 'But we are alive – we have bodies.'

'Yes, so have I,' I pointed out, 'But I have been dead for eighteen months.'

They looked at me aghast; one of them bravely asked if I could help them to escape from the island.

I said, 'Yes, at once,' and greatly to their astonishment, we floated out through the ceiling.

I heard one say, 'He must be right you know, I could never have done this before.'

On landing, they caught sight of a car on the wharf, and asked me what it was. I realized that they were still living in the fifteenth century, so explained briefly that it was a kind of travelling coach. They looked puzzled and asked where the horses were, as they saw it move without any. I tried to tell them that it was now several centuries since their death in the body, but they frankly refused to believe a word of it, so I said, 'Well, go off, and find out for yourselves.'

Coming back a little time later, they clung to me and said they'd seen no one they knew, the whole place was changed, and no one spoke to them. I explained that they were invisible to those in the body, being now in their spirit-bodies, but they couldn't take it, and kept on reverting to their old lives.

Then suddenly, one of them stood up and groaned, 'Look look, there is Alexis.' And looking in the same direction I saw a man who might have belonged to their period. He came towards us and on recognizing them, he said with horror, 'You! You here? I thought I'd left you behind forever.'

My party were cowering in terror by this time and I was trying to shield them. I asked the stranger what he had against them.

'Against them? They are the executioners. I was one of their victims.'

Don't worry,' I replied. 'They are now your victims. Look at them.'

And with that he laughed and said, 'Yes. It's all over really. It was just a sense of the old bitterness. Now it has passed, and I will help them.' Which he proceeded to do, and gaining courage, they left me, to follow him.

*Two letters from Joe (Cynthia's brother, Sir Alvary Gascoigne)*

## THE TYCOON

I asked Pat what happens to the millions of people who come over with no one in their entourage to help? Her reply was: 'Come and see.'

So I found myself in a rather rich house, with an old man just passing out of his earth body. He had been a real tycoon in industry and very rich. His poor old wife couldn't face life without him. He'd always done everything and now she was alone. I sensed that they had no children, and he'd been so successful that he'd alienated most of his contemporaries, and there he stood outside his body, a grey, frightened individual completely alone. . . .

I went up to him and spoke some sort of a welcome to show he wasn't quite alone. He heard me, looked round the room and merely grunted, 'How the devil did you get in?' I laughed and tried to explain, pointing to his corpse on the bed. 'What have you done to me?' was his next remark. 'Have you killed me?'

'No,' I repeated, 'you must remember your illness.' He nodded. 'Well now you have died according to the doctor, but you see there is no death, only a change of body; how do you feel?'

'I don't know who you are, and you've no right to be here, get out.'

'Of course, if you say so,' I replied, 'but then you will be *quite* alone.'

'No, I didn't mean that, you can stay, you are only a voice anyhow.' Then he began to see me, 'Oh you're not only a voice – you are a man! Well how do you see me and my wife doesn't? Can you tell me that?'

'Yes,' I replied, 'you are an etheric now; you have left your physical body for ever.'

'That can't be true, this is just a dream and a very worrying one too, I'll wake up in a moment.' Then he went over to the bed and tried to overlay his body, but it was cold and repellant. 'Can't do it,' he said in desperation. 'Well come and help me whoever you

47

are. Anyway, I'm *not dead*.' But he was so exhausted that I was able to persuade him to lie on a sofa in his own room and in a moment he was asleep.


*[Later]*

I want to go back to my tycoon whom I left asleep on the sofa. I knew he would wake before his funeral and need help. So I kept a tab on him as Pat calls it and sent out messages to find out his condition. When people began to come into his room I feared he would wake, and so he did. Looking up suddenly he saw me and said, 'Hello, you here again. Who the devil *are* you?'

'Not the devil,' I assured him. 'Just a guide to explain and help you to deal with this new situation.'

'What situation? Oh yes I know you said I was dead. Well that's a good joke; I'm fine, simply grand, better than I've been for years. I haven't woken up as fresh as this for a long time.'

'Wouldn't you like to come outside and have a breath of fresh air?' I suggested.

'No I'd prefer to stay here. If as you say I'm dead, then I'll prove to the wife that I'm nothing of the sort.'

'Well,' I said, 'Go and try, but remember you are in a different body now and she can't see you.'

'Well that's as may be; I don't feel ghostly or airy fairy – I'll have a try.' So saying he got up and started to walk out of the room swaying badly. I took his arm.

'What's wrong with me? I've not been drinking, but I can't walk steady.' I explained that he had to learn to walk with his new body.

'Oh stop talking all that trash, here I am just as I was in my old pyjamas, there's no change.'

'Well go on and see,' I urged.

The door was shut, he seized the handle and tried to turn it, but his hand slipped off the polished surface, and the effort he made sent him through the door! That shook him. The stairs were the next obstacle, he held on to me and floated down quite comfortably. 'Like sliding down the banisters as a boy,' he murmured. We came to his wife's sitting room. Again the door offered no barrier, but he began to feel uncertain of himself.

48

'Hettie!' he called as he saw his wife writing letters, and crying as she did so. 'Hettie, don't cry love, I'm all right.' No movement, no reply; he went closer. 'Hettie don't you hear me?' He shook her arm, or tried to, but again he could get no grip. He yelled into her ear, but she took no notice. He became exasperated. 'Has she gone daft?' was his next question.

'No, but *you've* changed. You've passed through two doors; you floated down the stairs, and now you expect her to hear your voice which has no material vibrations. Go up to that large mirror and breathe on it – can you see your breath?'

No! But what am I to do? Thanks goodness you *are* here, I can see you and you can see me and hear me, otherwise I'd go mad.'

'Do you know or care for anyone who has already died?' I asked him.

'Oh yes plenty, but how do I reach them?'

'By thinking of them, your thought calls them.'

'That doesn't seem sensible, but I'm in a fair do – I'll follow your instructions.'

I urged him out into the garden, I wanted to get him away from his weeping wife. There were some chairs under a tree and I said, 'Sit down and think.' He sat, but not on the chairs: he floated above them and complained that I'd put one of those damned air cushions under him. All the same he was quieter, and he soon began to think of his old friends.

'There was George who died last year . . . No he had a terrible illness, he couldn't be alive now.'

I said, 'He is, just think of him and call him.'

So he did, 'George, this is silly but I'd be right glad to see you.' And in a few seconds the form began to appear of a quite healthy middle-aged man. 'Oh George,' he gasped, 'how did you get here?'

'I heard your call,' was the simple answer. 'Have you come over too Rob? Well that's great.' And for a few moments the two old friends compared notes and were so relieved to find each other, I thought I could leave them, but Pat said, 'No, you've got to see Rob asleep first, then you can go.'

Their conversation rumbled on, Rob becoming calmer and more content and eventually he slept. I turned to George and said, 'What about you, are you an established etheric?'

'Well not quite, but I'm getting accustomed. I'll look after him. Thank you for looking after and helping old Rob. You know he's not a bad sort really. . . .'

I know you are wondering why in the world, and throughout the world you are having so many catastrophes.

Don't you see the answer?

The world has gone completely, or almost completely materialistic. They worship money and power on this plane and on the lowest level, and so to break their mad rush, groups of people have to be withdrawn suddenly, so as to *shock* those who remain into some sort of fear or a questing state of mind.

I was in Douglas when this awful thing happened, and it was terrific, and if seen from your side only it was horrific. But there was another side.

Flo* was there in charge of the children, and she got them away with a rapidity that had to be seen to be understood. She literally ripped off their etheric bodies, (like shelling peas as she put it).

Children can be so amazed by being shown a vision that they are quite impervious to physical pain. They allow their consciousness to flow into the exciting beauty which is flung within scope of their vision, and while this moment lasts the bodies are separated, and Flo took them all far away from the scene in the twinkling of an eye.

But, for the anxious parents, it was quite another story. I went with a young couple in search of a child of four or six, who'd been left in the children's playroom perfectly happy while they sauntered off elsewhere. Then it happened! Their first thought was 'The child!' – and they separated and rushed back by different routes. The mother got there first and found the child's body, and in a wave of deep emotion passed out of her own body almost at once, and was able to follow the tiny trail of the child's vibration and catch up with Flo's party including her own child. She had felt the burning, suffocating power of the fire, but her intense agony over the child had made her indifferent to it; and then suddenly it ceased, and she was *free*, and following a trail that only her finer body could detect.

Flo welcomed her at once, and placed her own child in her arms

* Florence Nightingale who was Cynthia Sandys' first cousin twice removed (her grandmother's first cousin).

saying, 'This is lovely, now you are together for *always*.' The woman was dazed and delighted beyond words at finding the child well and happy, and saw no change in herself or the child.

'Now we must go and find Daddy,' was her first reaction after the relief from this intense anxiety had passed. But here Flo or one of the helpers intervened with: 'No, you must stay here with the child. Your husband will join you here; we shall find him.' So, content for the moment and utterly exhausted by the emotion and all they had been through, both she and the child fell asleep.

· Tomorrow I'll tell you how we found the father.

*    *    *

Here is the story of the father of the child I told you about yesterday. I am going to pass his story down through you.

'We were properly frightened when the fire started. There were two ways of reaching the children's wing. I went one way and my wife the other. I soon realized there was very little hope unless someone had got the kiddies out already, but even that hope died when I got there, and found the remains in a molten condition. I saw there was nothing to be done but to try and help anyone I could. I found three children sheltering behind a wall and slowly suffocating from the smoke. I told them to lie flat and crawl with me towards the passage that might still be untouched by fire. We reached the entrance and the way ahead seemed possible, but the fire was roaring over our heads and as we reached the entrance a great beam or block of concrete fell on us. It was so sudden I was knocked out instantly and so were the children. The next thing I knew I found myself standing outside on top of the wreckage. It was burning furiously but it didn't touch me, and one by one the children joined me and cowered close together. We were all standing on the glowing embers, but we weren't being burnt. I couldn't understand it. I didn't dare to move as there was fire all round us and the children were terrified. I wasn't somehow, this was all so strange. Some queer draught, I thought, had taken the heat from the spot where we were, and if we could only stay quite still the fire might burn out, or rescuers reach us, so I told the children to stay quite still and wait. We did so – the fire blazed and we were all caught up in a strange way by the beauty of it, and out of the fire seemed to come shapes, and forms, and living people. Others joined us, seeing that we were unhurt, and we became quite a large group.

Then suddenly we heard voices calling us, 'Don't be afraid, walk out. Lift yourselves. You are free of the fire.' We took no notice at first – how could we lift ourselves out of the fire? Then a girl of about fifteen came up to me and said, 'This is exciting. It's like the astronauts walking in space. Have you tried it?'

'Well, no,' I said, 'how can I?'

'Like this,' and she took my hand and seemed to be stepping into the air. Quite unconsciously I followed her, and so did the children who were clinging to me. We were all a bit light-headed when we found ourselves walking in the air over the fire and looking down into it. Someone said, 'Don't look down. Look up.' I did so, and saw a whole mass of people like ourselves, actually walking on air! I thought: this is the strangest phenomenon. No doubt there is some quite natural, physical explanation of a gap in the gravitational pull caused by the fire. I was still very wary, I thought it might close in suddenly, and we should all fall down among the blazing ruins, so I told the children to hold on to me, and we would move as carefully as we could while this strange pocket of air held us, I hoped, until we were out of range of the burning building. We did so and moved quite easily. The current, as I supposed it was, seemed to be bearing us gently upwards. It was a very pleasant sensation. I was quite enjoying it and so were the children. Then a stillness came upon us. The roar of the fire and the screams and shouts of people died away and we were alone in space. . . . This was rather terrifying. What should I do next? We seemed to be quite a height above the ground. How could I get down safely with the children? Whenever I tried to drop down, my efforts were firmly resisted. I was growing desperate. Were we sailing off to the moon on some strange current of air? Then I began to hear voices telling me not to worry. I could see no one at

53

this stage, and I thought I must be imagining things, or getting delirious. The children were quiet and looked confident. 'Let yourself go. Relax. You are in safe keeping,' was shouted into my ear, and a short time after that I began to see we were in a large party being escorted, if you can call it that, on and on, into another layer of ether. I longed desperately to feel firm ground beneath my feet. 'You will soon,' said the same voice, and then my hand was seized by a firm grip, and before I knew what was happening, we were among trees and flowers and standing, as I'd hoped, on firm ground in a sort of garden.

'Where on earth have we got to?' I asked.

'Well, you'll see,' said the voice. 'It's not exactly on earth any more.'

Good heavens, what was the chap saying? Had I gone mad? The children were delighted. They'd left me and were running wildly about, exploring the garden. Then suddenly, in front of me, I saw the form of a man. He seemed to grow into my vision. At first only a blurred object, which crystallized into a human form.

'Who are you, and where am I?' I asked in amazement.

He was still gripping my hand, 'Take it easy son,' he said. 'You've passed over. You and the children have reached the next stage of living, you are now what the world calls dead.'

'Dead,' I screamed, 'but we can't be.'

'No,' he smiled, 'There is no death. That was one of the many illusions that we all find on coming over.'

'But,' I said, 'if I'm dead, so are my wife and child, I know, I saw them.'

'They are no more dead than you,' he said quietly, 'but at the moment they are sleeping off the exhaustion of this tremendous experience, and you and the children must do the same.'

I suddenly realized that I was dead beat. The children had already come back to me and were lying asleep like puppies on the ground.

'You seem to know all the answers,' I heard myself saying weakly, and with that I lay down and slept too.

*A letter from Patricia written at Pergamon, where her Mother and Joe were obliged to stop because their car broke down. Pergamon was the site of Aesculapius' ancient Place of Healing.*

I do want to tell you more about Aesculapius and what I saw. It was all so simple, thorough, and absolutely lovely, because the first cause of health lies in happiness, mirth and laughter, which we call morale.

I saw the most hopeless-looking cases staggering in; they were first received by a clairvoyant priest who could sense at once if they were actually dying and their hour had come; if so he took them to a lovely place where hypnotic sleep was given them if the end was already on the way. (That means if the aura had the 'passing light' – that is the circle of light which enters when the 'call' has been sent out for the spirit to return.) If this state was already in being, they hastened the light by strengthening the spirit force, but if the light was not there, they began the treatment.

I did not see any failures, but there must have been some who fell back into the old ways of thinking. I found children as usual were the best patients, they had no set ruts of thought to be erased from their minds. I followed a little girl who I think must have had polio; she was quite paralysed, I thought she looked a hopeless case. The priest looked very carefully into her aura and murmured 'We may be just in time.' She was carried to the 'lustral spring' and bathed in it; this seemed to ease her a little; then she was given light hypnosis to which she responded immediately, and was laid on a bed of springy herbs (a sort of heather) with a soft wool covering, and she slept.

I waited to see her wake up; she did, some hours later, stretched her poor crumpled limbs, opened her eyes and smiled at me. 'You are well,' I said to her spirit, 'quite well.' The priestess came, and gently massaged her all over, and enquired about her dreams.

She replied, 'I have been in a lovely place, full of children, some older, some younger, but they were all ill to start with, and then they all got well and began running about.'

'Just like you,' said the priestess, 'So now off you go,' and she took her hand, and the child sprang up and went skipping out into the sunshine.

The priestess turned to me and said, 'Isn't it easy with children? Now you shall see a harder case.'

This was a woman of about sixty who was suffering from some long-standing complaint of the stomach, I couldn't diagnose it, but she arrived in great pain, and was given the same treatment as the child. She awoke refreshed but still in pain, and rather disappointed and despondent. 'But we haven't started yet,' said my charming priestess, 'You must eat now and then we shall all pray together, and you will be told in prayer how to sow hope into your mind, hope, then faith, and lastly conviction. Those are the steps you are about to take.'

'But I've had this trouble for years,' she bleated, and seemed very anxious to tell us more!

'Don't think of the past, think only of the future,' said the priestess very firmly as she threw out her own aura in prayer.

This was a new experience for me, the woman tried to pray and relaxed, so that I could see her grey aura was open to reception. The priestess threw out a great golden circle of light which enveloped the patient with a golden glory of force. I could feel it so strongly, I was almost overcome myself. After a few moments this ceased, and the priestess asked the woman, 'Do you feel any better now?'

'Yes, I tried to pray, but I found I could only feel a warmth coming in through my head and neck. . . .'

'That was right – now think about that warmth as healing.'

The woman was unconvinced but interested.

'Now I am going to draw that power right through you to cleanse whatever may be keeping you from health.'

'Will it hurt?' asked the patient.

'No, of course not, no one is ever hurt here,' was her sharp reply. 'Now let yourself think of sunshine, and if you are fond of music, think of a tune, go on repeating the tune all the time, sing it; or if you like recite poetry, but keep your mind away from illness.'

The woman understood and began moaning out some dreary ditty which kept her mind away from the trouble; after a time she grew sleepy and soon dozed off.

I waited and when she woke she was decidedly better, stronger, younger, and more alive.

56

'I do feel better,' she allowed, 'I believe it is doing me good.' The priestess came to her and asked if she had been dreaming?

'Yes,' – but it was all a sad story of poverty and sickness, which was suddenly converted into light.

\*     \*     \*

Ma, can I go on about Aesculapius and the healing? My woman patient was obviously getting rather excited; she confided to me that she had been terrified of coming. She'd been told that she would be left all alone in a black tunnel! 'But this is so different, and everyone is so kind.' The priestess told me that she had been trained by Hygeia in the early days of healing, and had come back twice in subsequent lives to continue this work. The great Hygeia I also saw in the etheric; her power to heal was quite simply love; she had taught my priestess how to throw out the encircling wave of love power. 'Now this is not easy with difficult characters,' she confided to me, 'With children it is so easy, and they respond so quickly, but with the irritable and the disgruntled it is sometimes very hard; so one has to be quite impersonal.'

Now to go back to our patient – she was sleeping on a pallet bed, very soft and comfortable. Bread, fruit and milk was brought to her when she woke; she looked at them sourly and asked for something I didn't understand, but the priestess shook her head, adding 'Not during treatment, only the simplest foods, massage, rest, sunshine, music and the theatre. . . .'

'Oh but I couldn't walk there, the pain would come back again.'

'Just try a few steps and see.'

So she did, the theatre was close, we got her a seat, and she came out in fits of laughter! The treatment continued, sleep, massage, rest in the sunshine, drinking and bathing in the lustral water, music, colour, and *fun*.

'This is a real holiday for me,' she observed one day, when I'd

57

begun to think of her as cured, but the priestess said, 'No, if we sent her away now she'd fall back into the old way of thinking; now she must break completely with the past and go through the tunnel of fear into the light of knowledge.'

It was all explained to her quietly that one night, and she would choose her own time, she would meet the hypnotic priest who would put her into a receptive state, 'not trance', and lead her to the mouth of the tunnel where the whispering water would accompany her, and voices from the darkness would at intervals repeat the all powerful mantrams of health which in her receptive state would sink into her aura and bring complete conviction that health was the normal, natural condition, and that all other conditions had been entirely erased from her consciousness.

She was rather nervous about this treatment, so no one hurried her; she lived happily in the atmosphere of healing and rest, until one day when she began to feel she must get into touch with her family and go back to ordinary life. Gathering herself together she went to the priest, passed through the tunnel alone and at night, and came back to us tremendously bucked at having achieved this last test; she left us in a blaze of excitement with the conviction that she'd been completely cured.

*Some extracts from letters from Sally upon a variety of subjects.*

## WORDS OF POWER

This is a new line for me altogether. In the beginning God created words of power, and they were used down the ages in varying degrees. The Egyptians used them, the Greeks, the Chinese, the Indians – but they lost the knowledge of the power of words as they became separated from Divinity. When this happened, words fell back into being just words. I was made aware of words soon after I came here. I heard a circle reciting a votive prayer: and then I realized the meaning of Church services – e.g. when we all say the Lord's Prayer together. I saw the atmosphere round this circle glow – and then become threaded with light. And as I watched I heard the mantram they were reciting repeated again and again like an oratorio. I never before understood the meaning of repetition – especially when this is sung, not said.

One day, the power in the spoken or the sung word will return; and D. is one of the group detailed to help carry this out. I asked him if I could join the group – he looked at me and said, 'Sing!' Though D. has only been over a short time he is already united to at least a part of his greater self, and this part spoke through him and told me I could do it. 'But you must go out and practise with the knowledge that every sound you make is reacting somewhere upon someone.' I tried to think high notes and low notes. And then he said, *'Speak*, don't sing. And let me see your voice record.' I couldn't think what to say! So I fell back on poetry and recited Rupert Brooke: I think it was *Grantchester*. He stopped me and said, 'Well done, you've *seen* the poem, I could live it with you. That is exactly what I mean. Take any poem or song that gives you a picture, and see that picture with all the strength and emotion of your personal imagery. And then you will bring life back into words.'

The second time I tried, I not only said it all in my mind, but it was laid out plainly in front of my vision like a TV film in colour. I said, 'Can I make others see this?' 'Only if you can infuse their minds and they are capable of drawing in from your vibs.'

But this is just the beginning! So now I am launched upon a quite new venture. *And the Word became Life and lived among us.* Is that right?

Don't cast out the churches! They too are changing. I went into one, and found it crammed with living entities from our plane. I said, 'What are you doing here?' and they said, 'We are a body of old church workers. Oh, we were a dull lot,' one woman told me. 'But we had this vague feeling for something undefined that drew us to this church and others. And now to our astonishment we found on coming over that there were two rays – just two – that were acting as magnets. One was very ancient and pre-Christian, but so powerful that I couldn't even stand up in my ether body. When I was near the ray, I had to lie flat and be consumed and absorbed by it, and used for entering into the auras of others near. I asked what this ray was, and I was told it was the first ray of creation; and into this was absorbed those lesser rays formulated by all the early creeds of Sun and Serpent Worshippers. I was horrified and said, 'Oh! But I couldn't *touch* any pre-Christian ray." Whereupon I was laughed at and shown that these were the stronger forerunners of the Christ ray: they were the John the Baptists on a vast scale.

'I felt a little better, but still rather bruised in my mind, until they allowed me to feel the full force of the Christ ray; and then the bruises were healed and I became oh! so radiant, and had almost lost the dullness of my old personality. And I kept on laughing at the fact that we all – rather staid, narrow Church people – had to go through this baptism of the pre-Christian rays before the Christ ray was permitted to touch us. Now it seems so natural; but then I could hear the moans of those suffering (so they said) from the idolators.

'And now we see and are deeply grateful for all those stumbling steps humanity had to take before this wonderful Christ era came into being. Thank you for letting me say all this.'

You've no idea what a funny frowsty little party they must have been. They showed me their old selves on the Akashic records; and at the same time we both explored these wonderful first-Christian rays. I've never penetrated so far back in time; and oh! the fire and strength and absorption of these rays that created the dinosaurs and all the fossilized fish and plants that we know; and set in motion life on the material plane.

# THE SHEEP

I have always loved animals as you know, but never really had time to consider them very carefully. Now, your brother Joe, Cynthia, has opened my eyes to the other lines of evolution which they all take. It is so fascinating. I've been trying out the feelings of cows and rabbits – and then we took young things, such as lambs and foals. But they were too instinctive. So we turned to the old men and women of their race. The sheep were extraordinarily wise, particularly the mountain sheep in Wales. I thought it would be fun to go to places I knew, and see how the sheep felt there. They have a weather sense that mocks our weather men into fits. They can foretell a whole season! Just think of your long range forecasts – always wrong. But the dear old ewe whose sense-body became mine for a space told me that Election Day was going to be fine and dewy: dew is important, she said, in every sense. The dew released a lovely freshness into the air, and this in turn affected mankind and sheepkind.

I followed her life among her lambs, and her feelings when they were parted; these were far more philosophical than ours. She knew that her lambs would be killed; and that *she* would be in the end, and that until then, she must bear, and bear and bear more and more lambs. I asked her if this was not a very sad future to look forward to, and she said, 'No. I love the pastures and I love the lambs. And when they die they go on.' She didn't define that, but obviously any thought of death as finality had never occurred to her.

Then I went on to a mare and a foal. The mare was relaxed and happy and entirely centred on the foal, and thought my intrusion an awful bore. She wanted to go on having constant love scenes with her foal, who was too excited at being born to be coherent.

Above all, these two pasture-loving creatures got an immensity from the grass. It was life, beauty, comfort, eternity – and a constant flow of pleasure to them on quite another plane.

Animals are *conscious* of a soul. Do you realize this? Immortality is so completely a part of their divine being – yes, divine being – as to be unnecessary (for them) to comment on. They know they will go on. I wish you could realize the delightful calm wisdom of my old ewe. I felt she must have been in the stable long ago, and welcomed the baby Jesus.

*This letter is Sally's first report on a friend for many years, a distinguished historical biographer. Throughout her adult life, she had stubbornly refused to consider the possibility of survival of physical death; and, to the end, set her sights upon recovery from a long and painful illness. R.L.*

## AN INTELLECTUAL FRIEND'S AWAKENING

Now I must tell you about H. Well! She has not accepted any change at all. I sat with her when she woke and said how glad I was that she had joined me. From the sound of my voice she thought I was you. Then she asked for her pen and papers, which of course I gave her; but the substance has changed and she felt the difference and grumbled that I hadn't found the right pens. 'These are all *flabby*. I can't write with this pen. What *are* you doing?'

I took the pen and wrote quite easily; but her mind was completely orientated to the material. Then she suddenly said: 'What's that noise? It can't be birds, can it?'

'Yes,' I replied, 'They are all round you.'

'Oh! Not in my room, I hope? But I rather like hearing them. Ros dear, can you get me some *food*? I'm so hungry.'

'What would you like, darling?'

'Oh anything. You know, just a few snacks.' So I tried to reflect the last type of goodies you had brought her. She looked at them rather disdainfully, and said: 'You've been very quick. Is there a new shop near here?'

I tried to explain that shops were not necessary on our plane, but she merely thought I'd gone bonkers and passed it off with a smile.

'Are you feeling better?' I asked.

'Yes, yes, I suppose I am. I do wish I could get out of this house soon into the fresh air.'

'Well, why not?' I asked, 'Come with me. I'll take you into the garden.'

'What garden?' was her quick retort. She is quite alert! So at last I just told her that I was Sally, not Ros, and that she had left her poor sick body and joined us on this plane of health and perfection.

'Perfection! There's no perfection anywhere. Just a mass of half-truths and semi-perfections.'

I said, 'Not *here*.'

'But where is *here*? What are you talking about? I'm in my old room. What's the matter with me? I must be delirious.'

Eventually after a lot of cross-talk I persuaded her to come with me into the garden; and she kept on saying, 'This surely isn't Hyde Park? Or Hurlingham? Or any of the old Squares?'

'No,' I told her, 'You are in the outer courts of heaven.'

There was a long pause; and then her only remark before finally falling asleep was, 'But where is your Mother? I can't go on without her.'

# Part III

*The Glastonbury Scripts*

*This letter from Olga, Patricia's godmother, was written on the Tor in 1944.*

Oh, Cynthia, do you know where you are? This place is the centre of the old Atlantean teaching, and I am being shown through you the great influences that brought it into being.

These wonderful beings outstripped all other races in their quest for knowledge, and in doing so overlooked the need for spiritual advancement in themselves. I see many of these great beings around you here. Mountain spirits, creatures of marvellous beauty. They are quite unearthly, and belong to another range of evolution altogether.

Now, I'm going to ask you to go back into the Abbey grounds, and write with me there. This is too strong, I cannot direct the power.

*[C.S. then left the Tor and returned, as requested, to the Abbey grounds, where the writing continued.]*

Now I can write more easily. Here, there is a kindly softened power; it is entirely different. Now I must go slowly and explain.

I see this place as a network of forces all possessing different colours, mingling and intermingling like a cascade of water in the sunshine, but the colours do not merge, they remain unchanged, they weave their way in and out, some in unison, some in opposition to the rest, but mainly in conjunction with them in order to perfect the whole.

The atmosphere on the Tor was primaeval. Here it is the Christian and the mediaeval. The two powers form a contrast to each other, but we can if we will form a link through our minds between these two forces.

You and I have often lost interest in the Christian Church, because of its simplicity, and lack of technique as compared with the great eastern religions. They carried with them an immense load of philosophy, and like a goods train they had to move slowly. Into this slow evolving world came Jesus, the Christ. He came as

69

an athlete stripped of all but the essentials. Christ did not come in order to bring us another step further, but to leap forward into the unknown regions of the love planes.

It was as though the Great Spirit had suddenly grown impatient, and a bridgehead had to be won across the river of ignorance. Christ came as a commando equipped with one thing which he came to impress upon the ether: it was love.

His followers for many centuries tried to follow his example of simplicity. They had to remain aloof from other creeds while they were still struggling upon the slippery slopes of disbelief. These athletes who followed their leader had to ignore all detail and see only the goal that lay ahead.

Since then we have gathered knowledge and time has enabled the slow moving philosophies to catch up with the advance guard, and certain places have been prepared where the two worlds of thought and feeling can meet. This place and Iona are two of the meeting places where the ancient wisdom and the Christ love unite: not (fundamentally) the teaching, as Christ taught, but after centuries of pain, suffering, and disappointment, the essence of the original teaching has emerged; and here we find the Christ Ray enfolding the Abbey and all the ruined buildings.

The important point is that *now*, at this moment, the complete union of the two worlds is vital. It was effected once in the person of King Arthur and his knights, who, by the way, are as true as any other historical fact, but the world was unwilling to adopt his creed. He was killed, and his followers scattered, while the material age of thought flowed over his memory. But all the essential vibrations were locked away in the atmosphere until the time when they could be restored to the human race.

*This letter from Sally was written shortly after the death (in September 1968) of Wellesley Tudor Pole – following a message from him asking that C.S. and R.L. should visit Glastonbury together.*

I am often at Glastonbury, because I belonged there in one of my earthly lives. I was a very simple person living a primitive existence, but with some of the old learning. I only see small scenes which I can't piece together very easily. I am often in or near the Tor. I do not fear the Tor. I lived when it was first built and made into its present shape. I belonged to that very early race who knew how to use the elemental forces and continue life in complete harmony with earth. We have always loved Earth the Mother as the female side of God, the great nourisher and sustainer; so we couldn't bear to see Earth discarded. It was all rather childish, and there arose dissention which has wasted so much power. Now our task is to bring back those of the old race and blend their learning with all who understand like T.P. He was one of us then, and before the Tor was built.

*This group of letters from W.T.P. was written at Chalice Well in February 1969, when C.S. and R.L. visited Glastonbury in fulfilment of their promise to W.T.P.*

I'm a little strange to this new method of talking to you, my dear. Forgive me if I seem stiff, you know I could never say things before strangers; not that Sally, or even Cynthia come into that category. But we have shared so much so often in other lives. . . . I have a mass of material to discuss with you. It would take volumes!

We'll concentrate on Glastonbury. I woke up there on my second awakening after the 'second death', when I had really shaken off all the earth attachments – and I found a Glastonbury which was almost unknown to me. I didn't know my way about. Realizing it was Glastonbury on some other plane of vision, I waited for my understânding to pick up the vibration; and then out of the mists I found the Tor. For me this was the centre of power. It began long ago, and has now become attuned to human and Christian vibrations, which the Devic world had firmly held out against. I saw the old great Devic beings standing on the Tor. I had seen them before, but not clearly; now they were radiant and magnificent in all the ancient beauty of mind and power. Then, as I watched, they changed, and softened into the more humane Christ ray. I saw a turbulence of beauty glow in the valley, and reach up, enveloping the Devas – changing them with the love rays of the Christ power. This has nothing to do with the Abbey – it was almost in spite of the Abbey that the apricot light of Christ's aura grew and blended with the smoke-blue of the Glastonbury vibration. The two rays formed into a most astonishing pattern, resembling a huge flower with tendrils reaching out in all directions. I sat down and basked in the beauty and intensity of this experience. That, my dear, is all I can tell you today, because I have exhausted my earth vibrations. I will go on tomorrow.

\*     \*     \*

Thank you Cynthia, it's much easier today. I will even dare to call R. Alexias; that was her old name several times, because in pre-Christian days when one life succeeded another with far more rapidity, she kept on reincarnating in the same family! They knew when to expect her – him – whatever you like to call her – and they naturally repeated the name. Yes, they were tremendous lives, after a primitive fashion. We didn't get very much further in each life, because the light of evolution was going through a dark night – to be broken by the dawn of Christ's life on earth. I have now regained much of the knowledge which I had in my greater self; but only half-truths were filtered down to me in the last life, with many contradictions.

Now to go back to Glastonbury; it is and was our home in several incarnations; and I love it now with a strength unknown in my earth body. I returned, as I told you, and saw the great Devic spirits; then I entered the Christ ray, and called upon my sight to give me the true answer about Joseph of Arimathea and the Jesus story. That is the answer! It is part of the *Jesus* story. The Christ had not yet taken over the body of the boy who came to Glastonbury; but he was overlighted by this great Spirit. At this time, there were also other Masters preparing Glastonbury for the revelations that were to come later. I do not think Glastonbury is meant for a dramatic role of tremendous visions. It is the slow and constant seeping through of Spirit which has impregnated the whole area. And the constellations! I want you to know a little more about them; they are important because from each group of stars a certain area was chosen for their focussing point. They were to blend and bring the rays from outer space and from the other Masters working there, into relation with the Christ ray. We shall gradually introduce you to the other Masters there, who, like Christ, were the embodiment of Divinity in other planets through-out the universe. So you see, Glastonbury is not confined to Christ: *we are there in touch with interstellar Divinity*, which has a very different vibration altogether, and must be accepted with great care after meditation and assistance from this side. I want you to feel that here and at Iona we are the lighthouses for this planet. There are lesser ones; but here the great ones from all the divine planes, keep in touch.

It is only natural that this spot, chosen before time, should become the centre of Devic power, and then of Druid power, and so on. . . . But Sally is beginning to nag at my elbow, and say I have used enough power, and I haven't even answered your questions! Joseph of Arimathea – yes, of course he came, and his earth body rests here.

# THE SAPPHIRE BOWL

My very dear Alexias, how can I tell you about the sapphire bowl? It is not for me to explain its beauty or its mission. I know when I touched it *[He means when he first touched it in the body. R.L.]* that quite a new vibration flooded through me – one that was not wholly on the Christ ray. Now I know it was meant to be the keystone for interstellar Divinity; but before it had become materialized the Devic powers of a lower vibration took charge; and because of this, it had to be lost and buried near water, so that the water vibration could cleanse and heal the damage caused. I had to find it again and hold it secretly within the aura of my own security. All of this I knew in a half sense. I acted under direct instinctive direction; but the final use – if anything can be called final – is quite beyond me. I know the metal was placed for a purpose, to draw the mineral world into contact on all planetary planes: this I have been shown. The celestial power in the glass is beyond me to explain or understand. I was told to find and hold secretly this weapon of superb power, and that a day would come when it would be used to immense purpose on earth.

*[In answer to a mental query from C.S.]* No, it is not specially of healing value: that may be a side issue; but primarily it is an awakening symbol. Once the initiate is fully tuned in to receive this very high vibration, he (or she) will awaken to the interstellar power of communication and interception of thought.

It provides such a curious thing in the aura; it become almost sticky, so that vibrations can be caught when they would otherwise flow through without leaving a mark of any kind. This is all I can tell you at present. . . . I am being shown how to regain much which I knew of old. It is a fascinating existence and one I long to share with you; and I will as far as I can. Now I've said my say for now, and with deep love and gratitude for all that you have given me I will make my bow and pass the pencil to a very impatient Sally. Always your faithful T.P.

\* \* \*

*[Later: written in the Upper Room.]*

*[T.P.]* Yes, yes, I am here in this room created with so much care and thought; Alexias, I knew you and Cynthia would come and speak to me here and make me feel that I have left some particle of value to mankind. One feels after the reviewing of one's life how little one has done with all the opportunities that came one's way. . . .

*[He continues at some length reviewing his 'lost opportunities' and his 'faults' (as he sees them) with the most touching humility, humour, and clear sightedness. He stresses the importance of laughter, adding,]* I didn't laugh enough! I was given a sense of mirth and wit and could use it if I wished; but I never cultivated it, and became austere and rather sad. Don't do anything of that sort, Alexias. Never quench the laughter that comes even from silly jokes. . . .

*[Sally followed him with a longish letter, ending,]* . . . so I can't tell how much T.P. is teasing you and how much is true.

Now Mummy darling we must work hard tomorrow. I am trying to prepare to give you more in the writing. This is such a wonderful place, and one could say anything – but there is a kind of censorship. I suppose you are meant to find out a lot for yourself without a short cut like this. . . .

\*     \*     \*

*[Next day.]*

*[T.P.]* Good morning, girls! Well, here you are – a lovely moment of writing with you both – a triumvirate! – always a very strong number to attack a problem. Of course I am fresh to all this and slow to register the great inner meaning of all we find and know, and refind and recollect at Glastonbury. This house is very fortunately on the outer ring of the modern destructive thought-process which goes on within the centre of the town – or village as it really is. There is a great difference in the vibration between a village and a town. The wholesome vibration of the soil is all

76

important, and it is that which will save Glastonbury. It is still a village as far as the vibration goes.

Now to the Bowl. Yes, it is an intrinsic symbol of Christliness. So advanced is the vibration that it will not impinge upon your lesser auric vibrations, but reaches its fulfilment in your auric self. In this it glows and burns and will have an increasing value in the unfoldment of your powers of perception – ESP and so on. I cannot yet classify the uses for this bowl. I think at the moment – *repeat, at this moment* – I think it is meant to radiate from here within our solar system and perhaps beyond; but I have not yet adventured into the beyond. I am still amazed and mystified by all the different planes of thought and feeling. I am quite unable to classify anything yet. You must take all I say with a spoonful of salt – good strong salt. I came over thinking I knew something of what I could expect, but I assure you, it is all beyond and beyond anything I could devise out of a fairly active imagination – and there is so little that can be expressed in words. Our communication with you through this channel is the way in which we can stress our immortality – our unchanged selves as individuals, as beings who love and laugh and suffer. In all of these things we are quite unchanged, and I feel, at present, unchangeable; and that through the force of our love we should be able to influence your finer bodies into a tremendous growth. This is vital and urgent. And now I see the time factor in quite a different light. It is not events which are coming to you, it is *you* who are drawing *them* towards your own plane. The meeting is inevitable; and we who have already been granted the body of light can do a lot through *reflection*.

We cannot give orders or instructions from here – perhaps later, I don't know yet. But on seeing you with my new visual senses I am amazed at the growth you have made towards the taking over of your next bodies; and I know anything I could do to help would only come through your own channels of perception. People only learn what they already know in embryo – and the rest is completely superficial.

\*　　\*　　\*

77

*[Sally]* I stood by watching you handle the Bowl: it's wonderful to see your finer bodies prick up their ears, so to speak; and coming close to watch and listen, I sensed a soft musical note being transmitted all the time. You don't hear it – you only feel its warmth – but it's very apparent to us: just as the light I see contains presences around the Bowl: very old ones, sheaths of discarded personalities. These must be broken up and revisited by their own advanced owners of another life. They are the makers of the Bowl in the distant past. They are holding it and have been the defenders of it for many centuries. Now the time is at hand when those individuals have reached the stage of advancement when they are able to return and free the Bowl. These 'sheath' presences are necessary because without them it would never have re-materialized; but in their present state they retard advancement – no, that's wrong – they *curtail its penetrating power*. All this is *meant*. The timing is perfect. Too many people are reacting in a superficial way, and we want to bring those of deeper initiation in touch before the great awakening comes.

\*      \*      \*

*[T.P.]* Yes, I am here and anxious to write a little more. My dear Alexias, you have worked for me in this place that I love so deeply and I am very close to you here. I feel what we wrote together in *A Man Seen Afar*\* doesn't go far enough. You told me so; but I was always afraid of giving wrong information. Yes, I have erred on the side of saying too little. I am interested to hear that all my bits and pieces are being collected. I hope they will have some message for those who read them. . . . . I am delighted with the sense of strength I am experiencing, and the elasticity of my brain gives me enormous pleasure.

\* Neville Spearman, 1965.

I am engaged upon the Tor. Cynthia, you are right; so much hinges upon the feeling up there. People of power are always drawn to places of this nature, and their psychic vitality is stepped up; of course this means the negative side too, and this always has to be converted. In Jerusalem, in Iona, in all the places of power we have the counterweight of negative power to convert and transcend: that is our job with the Tor also. I have been up there and I talked with the guardians. There are several different layers of vibratory beings there. It is ringed by the friendly Devas – but those in the centre are strongly sexual and belong to the most ancient rites of the very early magicians. I belonged to a sect of this branch long, long ago – so I can make contact with them I find I was here almost at the beginning of this power centre, so it is my particular work now to restrain, convert and transcend the so-called evil. *There is no evil* – that *must* be accepted. There is a primitive force which is mainly sexual, gained through the blood of the sacrifice. This has been paid in full during the last two wars. All that bloodshed on our battlefields – shed in sorrow, pain, misery and hate, must all be used – I repeat *used*. Blood holds all the human aspirations, the best and the worst: but the best are transcendent and will overcome all the rest. I have my links from World War I: I have seen and shared in the turmoil of spirit, so in my small way I make contact with the whole; and through the power of that bloodstream, I am now treating the Tor. One must use the same vibration to cure as that used to invoke in the beginning. I am now gaining an immense army of people who gave all during war, to go with me, not only to one Tor but to many other places of like vibration. When you think of me, think of a stream of sacrificial power flowing through my fingers, my feet, from my head, in fact all the points of power, and see this taking form to convert the Tor and to resolve the quarrels and animosities among our best and dearest in this lovely, loving place.

\*     \*     \*

*[Sally]* What is true? Well, most of it I think. The Christ ray is certainly very strong here and Joseph of Arimathea – and all his followers – and King Arthur and so on. Where they are all buried I don't know – St Joseph I think, near the original wattle church. The rays of Arthur are so strong one can't quite pinpoint his grave – and why should one? The power is here and all graves have served their purpose and are empty so far as these high Spirits go. Their power is all present.

\*     \*     \*

*[T.P.]* Now to the Bowl once more. Cynthia is quite right – this lovely beautiful thing has been misused. The power within it has been invoked for greed and all kinds of selfish reasons. But the mud and slime (you remember where it was hidden) were the symbols of the mental conditions through which it passed; and they have cleansed it to a great extent, though not wholly. Now, this is interesting because the lower vibrations contained in it give the Bowl the power to enter into the aura of quite uninvolved people, whereas the wholly purified Bowl would have been exempt. Good and less good are all tools and the fact that the Bowl was fashioned *after* the Resurrection is another curious item. Christ kept touch with his physical body for a much longer time than is usual. I see now, with my etheric sight, how he went about, appearing to many people whose names do not figure in the Gospels. So his physical touch can well have dwelt upon this lovely cup: and I am almost certain that it did. I am almost certain because the *physical* touch is important to all of you. He has, of course, often held it within his etheric touch, and here again I feel the link with human greed is not out of place; it puts Christ into the picture of our human failings. Dear, dear Alexias, how we worry over trifles! I was one of those looking for chapter and verse, proof and detail when the great Chalice of Love was being poured over me. All the same we are meant to give and receive reasonable proof and to this end I will help all searchers.

# Part IV

## Father Andrew Glazewski

*Father Andrew Glazewski, much-loved Polish Priest, Initiate, Scientist, Musician, 'died' suddenly during a weekend Wrekin Trust Conference in November 1973. This letter came via C.S. four days later.*

The ecstasy of dying is something I can never express. It is suddenly like becoming light itself. It is so wonderful. It is heat and coolness. It is warmth in the mind. It is clarity of vision and understanding. It is like a clap of divine thunder, and hey presto, there I am out of my tiresome old body, leaping about in the glorious ether; and you've no conception of what dying is like. . . . It is a Communion, a Sacrament of living on a higher level – this is the most transforming experience that any mortal can attain. I am overcome with joy, pure *joy*.

May I write down exactly what I experienced?

The pain grew suddenly so bad that it seemed to burst or break something inside me – and I was suddenly *free – free* in the strangest sense. I felt for a moment inert and without power, as in a walking trance. I was above my body but still attached to it. I was sorry for it, it looked so helpless, almost like a child, and Gordon tried so hard to reawaken life in me again. Then I saw in his face that I had finished, and as you say 'dropped in my tracks'. Well, fair enough. I had tried to finish the course but no matter. So I accepted death, and as I did so the whole world changed. The room blazed with light. The books on the table, the chairs, even the carpet and the curtains, everything in that room was alive with love power.

I stayed quite still, quite close to my body, but I couldn't see it any longer; perhaps they had taken it away. It did not seem to matter to me any more.

I was at this time alone with *God*. . . . I had often tried to feel this at-oneness with the Divine, but never succeeded to this overwhelming extent. I felt like a piece of blotting paper that was being saturated with light. I waited in an ecstasy – every moment was beyond words. Had I been able to hold this in my body I could only have done so for a moment, but now I seemed to have gained a certain resilience, I became tireless in my power to receive.

83

How long it lasted I have no idea, but when I touched down again as you would say, I found all quiet and everyone in bed. Some were praying for me or thanking for my release. They made me feel very humble as I passed from room to room blessing them all in turn, not as I used to, but with a power quite outside my knowledge and experience.

All this time I had been content to feel and to glory in my personal relationship with Christ. Now I began to *hear*. At first it was quite low like a trickle of water – then it sounded like voices that were half singing. They had quite different tones from ordinary voices, but after a few moments I could both hear and understand, and I suddenly realized that they were speaking to me in Polish! I replied at once and found I was speaking to one of my greatest friends; a most advanced priest who had passed over during the war in Poland. I was overjoyed to hear him. It was then that I realized that I had not only shed my body completely, but I had received a new body, and acquired the power to use it straight away!

I asked him to come close and let me see him. To which he replied, 'Don't be in a hurry, you are newly born and cannot do everything at once. Here you will find many old friends and plenty of time for recuperation. Come, Andrew, I will show you.'

He took my arm, but still I saw nothing, I was hearing and feeling and seeing only this glowing light everywhere. I asked, 'Where are we going?' as we slid pleasantly through the light.

'I am taking you home to Poland and I am going to show what we on this side are doing in our country, because, owing to all the suffering, Poland has become a Holy Land.'

I will pass over the journey which delighted me. We reached the Poland that I used to know in my youth, now to be felt on the etheric plane. I was enjoying this when my friend said, 'Now we must go on to the next layer of the war years.' This was a terrible recapitulation of our sufferings under the Germans and the Russians – and then we went on to the next layer of the etheric, where those released from suffering were shown the land they must impregnate with *forgiveness*.

I was now seeing both the physical and the etheric planes. I was confused, but at this moment I turned towards the hand that held me, and I *saw* my friend! Not as he was during those last terrible days, but as he is now in the risen body of Christ's resurrection. I forgot Poland – I could only gasp with astonishment at the Goliath of light and energy whom I saw before me. Remember, I thought I was still in the little shrivelled body of Andrew, the counterpart to my old body, cleansed and enlightened, but still the same.

I was shattered at first: here was a strange being who felt and spoke like my old rather plain friend, but now he was god-like.

After a few moments of silence during which I was trying to size him up, he turned and laughed, his old ringing laugh! Well, I heard myself saying, 'Anyhow *that* hasn't changed. I must hold on to your laughter.' And so we gradually made contact again among the different vibrations

I was now beginning to see. I saw shapes and colours and out of these were formed bodies (ray bodies) of people I'd known and loved, not only in my past life, but in other lives. They were so kind to me, making me welcome, while I was still feeling like a Cinderella at a feast. I was still small and black in my old, old clothes. I began to resent their faithfulness; and then I looked at them with a sudden interest as I saw they were changing, and were somehow reflecting the colours from all around.

'You must hold on to your old clothes,' someone was telling me. 'They are your signature from your old life on earth. Wait and see how they will help you.' At this moment my clothes were reflecting the rays deep into my body. I could feel their warmth, it was like a love warmth. 'That is the residue from your aura that you were emitting from your physical body. It is very important that you should retain and enjoy the fruits of your earthly prayer and thought.'

Meanwhile I realized I was becoming clothed in a sort of golden cloth. It was warm to the touch and very soft. I was delighted with it, and apart from its warmth and comfort, I found it was actually shedding a light of its own. So I wasn't such a dull, black figure after all, and there was no need to feel ashamed: in fact, I became quite proud of my new body.

Then quite suddenly I was tired and they said, 'Sleep here, anywhere, rest for a short or long period.' I found myself lying on the ether, superbly comfortable, warm and contented beyond all description; and so I slept. . . .

*[Written some weeks later]*

I have been to my own Holy Land. It is redolent with the Christ ray. This will be my special undertaking at the moment. Just going to places I knew and giving them a boost.

Now to all of you who are trying to awaken faculties still dormant within, I would like to say, 'Call upon me, I can really help now, and I have found out that I can split myself up into many Andrews and they can all go out separately, and yet be used together, so don't think that Father Andrew is too busy and I mustn't disturb him! I am so alive and so awake and full of energy to be used and used, you can't call upon me too often.'

This is my first Christmas Advent over here. It is going to be most exciting. I am so grateful to God for calling me at this precise moment, when the earth sleeps under snow and frost and all the tiny nature spirits are awakening the roots, and bulbs and the trees. . . . Oh, the trees! They are pouring forth colour and scent and music. I am amazed and delighted! And how I love the little nature spirits – some I have never seen before in the snow and the hoar frost.

I do not need the long rest that so many insist upon. I have slept and shall continue to do so now and then – that is only when I am extravagant and uncontrolled, when I have absorbed more rays than I should – you see I am still rather greedy!

Give my love to them all.

Andrew

\*     \*     \*

My pen, I simply must write for a moment. I know your brother Joe and your husband, they are both working with me for the enlargement of consciousness: this is my aim, not only for all of you in the body, but for when you come over here.

There are a vast number of clever, intelligent people who have never grown the organ of *acceptance* – and here, too, they remain adament in their non-belief. This can only be changed by tuning in on their own level with the great Earth Spirit. All healing of the mind and body comes through the Earth Spirit, into which vibration we have been born again and again. Christ came to sanctify this great channel and to make it possible for power to pass to us through this medium. There are so few of us who can accept the Christ ray direct, it is so far beyond our range; but after allowing it to pass through the great Earth Spirit it becomes us. Do accept this. There have always been the few who can accept the sense of the Christos direct, but for those who can't, and they are in a vast majority, we must accept the medium of the Earth Spirit. Roc *[Ogilvie Crombie]* is here with me, and he asserts the same thing, he says, 'Pan came into my physical vision in order to make this more plain and concrete. God moves in a mysterious way, his wonders to perform.'

I am often working inside the earth with the great Mother Spirit. I came with your group to Everest, and I am now with Ronald, learning from him the intricate and lovely rhythm of the telluric currents. I will write more later. . . .

# FATHER ANDREW IN SPACE

Now I want to tell you about my life. I am not going away, but I am going on journeys and expeditions into the outer space and on to various planets and other places. I am frantically interested in the different forms of development and how we can help and be helped by them. I have been a long way outside our solar system, but it was on the next plane and I can give very few details. Words do not convey what we are able to accept mentally, through vibration. The effect on oneself is staggering. One's whole being seems to expand to receive this new awareness; and then when I pack myself back into my old shape and return to earth I feel constrained as though I were wearing clothes far too small for my immense body, but I now have no body as such. I am a group of vibrations for ever growing more complex and at the same time simpler. I am an awareness in the atmosphere. I know that sounds too diaphanous, but in reality I am far more concentrated in thought, and with this new etheric organ which directs and focuses the power it sends out. It also propels and I am able with help to decide upon the destination.

At first I was led by a party of old friends and people I've known both in Poland and here, and they took me with them. I was not able to travel alone and the effort of leaving the earth was intense. I love earth and she does not part easily with her children. Then a magnetic pull is very strong. I thought I should never make it . . . and then suddenly I am free. I am Andrew in outer space, outside the gravitational area which extends in the etheric much further than it does in the physical. Once outside, one is free on such a vast scale it is almost frightening, and from having been the large expanded Andrew I suddenly became a very small being, so tiny I hardly existed at all, but what was there was intense, frightened, but very full of curiosity. My friends also seemed small, but I was glad of their company and together we swung on through this delightful area of planets and suns.

We seemed to pass an immense number of worlds in all types of development and different grades of vibration. There were *colours* such as I have never seen before. I have no names for them, but they each had a different effect upon me and I began to grow again. It was like *Alice in Wonderland*. The colour was growing into the corresponding vibration to the worlds we were meeting on our way. I do not know what our destination was, but it was beautiful. It was not like Earth, hard and formed, but full of misty colours and the most beautiful beings.

I know all this sounds like a fairy tale and so it is – one scene after another of such breathtaking beauty that I began to feel I had reached the zenith of my power to accept. I pleaded for a pause, a rest, and then a homecoming. Suddenly I was Andrew again in my old personality, wanting only simple pleasures and acceptable beauty. This was beyond me.

I seemed to rest and sleep – and when I woke I had been carried home to my old pastures. So you see, life here is full of incident. But we take time to outgrow our old personality, if indeed we ever do.

Now I have written enough for one day. Goodnight to you both and thank you. I am so happy to be able to write this down. It helps me to think it over, and perhaps open some more channels of acceptance.

My love
Andrew.

Cynthia, I am glad to write with you here on Iona. What a place it is; you call it a 'thin' place, where the planes meet without a film to separate them.

I am delighted to be back again among your lecturers. Tell them not to be afraid to speak here in this wonderful medium of the Iona atmosphere, where all things can become true that have any truth in them, and those who cannot accept the truth should not come to this advanced realm!

Now, this island, it is indeed a rich place. You can only see a very small part, and perhaps feel the rest. I have been through Iona. I have entered the soil and the rock and been down to the very centre of the earth, where I have been constantly guided and helped by the great Earth Spirit upon whom rests the guardianship of these sacred places. I have met St. Columba! (Tell the artist who painted his picture that I recognized him at once from the likeness that she created). He is full of youth and fire and dynamic thrust. . . . Oh, how I long for you all to walk among us here as I do, meeting the Devas and the saints and the great Angel Spirits.

When I came back from my journey into space which I told you about, I was encouraged to learn more about Mother Earth before entering again into those high frequencies, so I came back to Iona, and here I found my exact vibration. I had been here before and I had accepted this as being true when I was still in the body. Iona has a very long history and goes back to the days of ancient continents; and we are homesick for the teaching and the power that was ours in another phase of living. But do not be discouraged. You are all here to awaken the Earth people and many are on the very edge of consciousness. You are all being used (if you co-operate) to assist in the greatest event in your planet's history. It may seem small and unimportant, but I can assure you it is not.

Built into each one of you here on Iona is a communicating set of vibrations, which you have been led here to vitalize and develop. There is no going back on the path. You must go forward and the veils between us are all lifting so rapidly.

Immediately beneath Iona there is a great dynamic pool of fire.

You feel this when you contact those warm spots on the island, and even if you do not feel them consciously they register on your finer body. I see Iona now as a great jewel, with light and colour radiating all round the world; and one of the tasks I have undertaken is to carry the flame of Iona and make the ray acceptable to those whose aura is ready for enlightenment.

I was with you all in the lecture room and I heard with very great pleasure all that was said. You may not agree, but I feel very strongly that you have now reached a point where illness and disease should no longer exist. Many are confusing their states of mind and rushing to drugs for a cure, when the Earth Mother could supply them far more easily if they could only turn towards her and the Christ ray. But they all want something new – something different, so I would urge them to seek help from the trees, the rivers and the sea. We have no greater healers. Christ used the mountain tops from whence he could draw all the earth and the sky powers into his range.


*[Next day, sitting on the shore of the western coast of Iona]*

You know, my dear Pen, this is a much better place to write and I'll tell you why. Straight in front of you, on that little knoll, are a group of Druids who were Columba's first friends. They are singing the old chants on the etheric which give power, health and enlightenment to the island. They are a wonderful group. One cannot easily tell a Druid from a Christian by the aura, except that the Druids have a deeper knowledge of the ancient wisdom, while the Christians have the Christ ray. This was very infectious, and the Druids were open to all infection of this kind; they were in Iona of a very high order of mystics.

I have been shown some of the secrets of Iona through them. One of these so-called secrets lies in a method of development taught by them which helped the soul on leaving the body to pass outside the earth aura and continue without reincarnation. This constant reincarnation was a terrible curse upon those who knew and accepted the hard lives that lay in store; so they sought by every means in their power to outstrip the necessity for physical life.

91

We don't understand this to the same extent now. Very few people accept the theory, and those who do find life a far less arduous lot than our ancestors of centuries ago.

So here, as in Chartres, Egypt and Greece, there was a school for the advancement of the soul upon other vibrations. Now we have outgrown that desire, and almost outgrown the need. We have the power to return as I am doing now, to learn and to teach, and at the same time to go out into space when we are ready.

You can have no idea how much ground has been covered by past generations; to us on earth it all seemed much the same, but to those who are now leaving the body they find a freedom beyond all conception awaiting them.

Now I want to speak about the greater self. This was a discovery for me of enormous importance. I had always glimpsed the possibility of there being a more advanced Andrew somewhere, but he was so elusive. I didn't really know how or where to look for him – then we met! I was slightly embarrassed. I was a new boy. He was myself grown wiser, but how were we to co-operate? He was tall – I was short. He was strong and athletic – I was wrinkled and puny. He was like an elder brother and yet he was me. I talked to him and asked how he could help me to become like himself, and then he took me in his arms as you would a small child and breathed on me – that was all, and I, Andrew, became as one with this great being. It is beyond understanding or explaining but it is true. We are only a very small reflection of the self we leave outside the earth body, and when we have accepted death and entered into the majesty of passing out of the physical, this wonderful enlargement of mind and spirit is awaiting us.

Now, to give you an example of how it works. While I, Andrew, was working away slowly in the body, learning to move without physical help, learning to see and hear, my other self was doing the same on a far larger scale.

So, when you make any slight effort on earth your greater body does the same, but to a vastly greater degree. All this is so exciting that I have used all our energy for today. Let us write again tomorrow.

Give my love to them all.

\*　　\*　　\*

92

Well, now that we are settled I really prefer a small room. We were always taught to meditate in our cells, and if not to build a dome of thought around us.

We have been closer today to the real centre of peace, and I would have you know that I have overlighted all your speakers in turn. Some of them brought very advanced spirit guides.

Now I want to speak to you about fields of force. You have been discussing the T-plane and others. That is right. You should begin to learn how to tune in to these different layers of consciousness. They were mostly names to me before I came over, but now, though I see that our deliniation of them was often faulty, the idea was right. Spheres of force are as geometrical as everything else you can name. Even the waves that seem so haphazard are fulfilling a pattern, and when you leave the earth plane and enter into these further realms, you find plane upon plane supporting and interlacing like the petals of a flower, or many flowers, each with colour, sound and form. It was very perplexing to me at first to be bombarded by so many with such gaiety and profusion.

I came to rest eventually at the side of the old Abbot teacher of my youth. He looked at me and said, 'Andrew, you have travelled far and been a torch bearer.' That surprised me. I thought I had gone in exactly the opposite direction from most of his teaching! He saw my embarrassment and laughed, and suddenly I saw that he was young and understanding, and had thrown off much of the old teaching, perhaps even as much as I had myself.

I pointed to the colour spheres and asked his help. He explained them to me in thought which is far too intricate for me to put into language. If Keith Critchlow were here I might be able to explain in symbols, but even they do not go far enough. You will have to reach out in thought beyond language before you can grasp the majesty and the meaning of the T-spheres.

But now to come back on to the earth plane. Here on Iona I see St. Oran. His chapel and his very personality are impressed here. What a marvellous directive for spirit growth. After I have probed as far as I can with my intellect, I go on with a new sense that I've been given something which exceeds intellect, but still thinks with a mind of a separate order; this is confusing, but very stimulating. I feel almost as though I were thinking alongside the Christed ones. But of course that is nonsense, and you must not encourage me in these extravagant ideas. Let us be practical. We must teach you first to see and hear. Once learnt, these lessons are of infinite value over here. I do urge you, with all your practical work, to pause and *feel*. Talk to the trees and flowers as I showed you: the greater your consciousness the more rapid your vision on coming here.

Now I've finished for today, but again tomorrow, please.

*      *      *

Cynthia, you have chosen a good place, or, to be exact, I've chosen it. I used to come here long ago when I was a humble Brother and escape from work, and come here to pray. I used this little wind-free corner from which I could see the far side of the island, the Land to which I had belonged – the Old Continent. Not all Iona is so ancient, but the far side most certainly is. How old I can't tell you and it is of no importance.

It is a beautiful island barbed with power and for this reason it must always be held in the love rays, otherwise it could become what I have seen happening in Poland and Russia, the most demoniacal centre.

I go back very often. It is one of my undertakings to free these misused centres. At present we can only amass the power for good against the day when Christ allows some human link, some Master in human form to win and transform the land. I am sure that day is not far off. The Masters are ready and awaiting their call for Russia, Poland and Czechoslovakia. Tribulation always brings strength, and you will see a tremendous awakening. But everything is always tied up with everything else. The more dynamic you can make Iona, the more advanced your group can become, the sooner all this will come about.

One great change has taken place within the last decade or so. It is *expansion* seen among all our groups. We no longer talk of the secret doctrines. We do not keep ourselves enclosed. We go out and give and share, and only by so doing can you develop and grow. You have seen what happened in Tibet, and before that in Greece and Egypt. Secrecy spelt detachment from earth and no further advance into mind or matter.

Now to go back to these fields of force that interest you so much. The L-Field and the T-Field.* They exist within the human body and also within all growing organisms. I am not sure if they do not also exist in the rocks. You must understand that everything that is God-created is alive, breathing, even thinking upon different levels, but keyed in to our evolution. We are responsible for growth or sterility. We can do so much more with our planet besides just looting and despoiling; and for that reason I am hoping that a moment will soon come when other beings will join you on earth to show and to demonstrate another way of living. I want you to reach out in thought to these greater beings by asking the Christ to bring his Christed ones within the earth vision. This is the plan for which we must prepare. It has been called the Second Coming. But it is not in the least like the original Coming of Christ. This will happen at first slowly, and all over the world people will appear possessing great dynamic force and power.

They will not command. They will keep in step with all of you in all the different walks of life, but slowly, gently, they will impress the love ray, and their gentle influence will be felt and guarded. Take this into your conscious mind and hold yourself alert to meeting, as you may well do, one of these advanced beings. The earth is ripe for this event, and there are an increasing number of awakened ones now in the body. See that the number grows and do not lose heart because of the apparent futility of your efforts.

Andrew.

* See *Blueprint for Immortality*, by Harold S. Burr MD, Neville Spearman, 1972.

# Part V

*Letters from Joe*
*(Sir Alvary Gascoigne, Cynthia's brother)*

*These letters are from my brother Joe, who served with the Inniskillen Dragoons in India before the first World War. He returned with his regiment to France in December 1914 and exchanged into the Coldstream Guards, with whom he served until the end of the war. He then took the examination for the Diplomatic Service, and served for the next forty odd years all over the world, including a long period in the Far East. He adored wild places, and had the true traveller's passion for challenging adventures and 'hair-breadth scapes'. On leaving Peking, he walked alone from Canton back through Yemen into Burma, following notes made by Colonel Pereira on his first journey. Joe would have loved to make more such journeys; also to do some serious climbing; but the stringencies of his career made this impossible.   C.S.*

## JOE'S DESCRIPTION OF HIS OWN DEATH

I had a good night of refreshing sleep on my last night on earth, and when you both came to see me I was in a state bordering upon pleasant relaxation. Every part of me seemed to be switching off gently, and when the last switch was pressed I suddenly found I was floating above my body. I made instinctively for the window; Mother was there, but I couldn't see her. She said my first words were: 'Thank God that's over – I never thought I should have lived through it,' whereupon she burst out laughing, and that was the first etheric sound I heard. I looked round and saw only you and Lorna*, obviously the laughter did not come from you. But in a few moments I could feel her arms round me and recognized her voice.

Nothing in life comes up to the immense joy of dying.

Death has been made such a bogey that it is only through suffering and great discomfort that we are persuaded to let go and co-operate with death. The body fights to retain life on any terms: it is the inborn instinct of the body brain, so we have to re-educate this body brain to the point when it will accept and relinquish its power without waiting for the spirit to be wrenched away through pain and disease.

* His wife.

You will find that more and more people just die in their tracks, which is the ideal way of leaving.

I told you that I had experienced a strange feeling of power that seemed to be drawing me out of my body during the last few days of my illness. I was hopelessly ill, and I knew it, so I welcomed this inrush of new life and let go very willingly. That was why I did not linger.

You must realize that when you have joined the 'Club' the passing cannot be very long delayed, and be ready to receive the power that draws you quite painlessly out of your body. It's the most beautiful and glorious thing. I see so many are prolonging their life quite unecessarily. If you give up the reins, as it were, to the great Creator, expressing your readiness, then life is withdrawn gently and lovingly, and the dossier of your earthly effort is closed.

We are not meant to suffer death. I am told that Christ by his suffering upon the Cross renounced the need for pain in passing through death. We now say relax and let life do with you what it will. Life commands; you agree and co-operate.

\*      \*      \*

This is tremendous. I feel slightly drunk and not quite steady on my feet but extremely happy and full of a sense of well being. I don't feel I should, but I do.

I was taken to Scarba. I said, 'Let's go round to the back of the island to look over towards Mull.' I became overpowered by the wonderful scents and sounds and the whole glistening beauty of it all; so I just sat down in the heather and tried to think back and remember how I'd got there and why I loved it so much. Mother and Douglas* and Pat all share this feeling. They brought me here to give me strength. It's the most wonderful tonic – no shot in the arm could be more effective. I stood up feeling as I used to long

* His son.

100

ago when we tore over the island to the pigeon caves at dawn. In fact I found we had drifted over to those very caves on the far side of the island overlooking Corrikrecken. How magnificent it all looked!

Then I remembered my life in phases as I grew up. The war, marriage, the children, the exam for the diplomatic service. My posts wandered slowly through my mind like a cinema. I went on working at one after another of our posts abroad, Paris, China, Hungary, Morocco, Hungary again after the war, Japan and Moscow; and on to the film came the sparkling figures of Lorna's dogs: everywhere they came but I couldn't separate them, until one poodle attached herself to me and I remembered Maruka. I must have called out 'Maruka' and suddenly she was beside me rubbing herself against me and showing great pleasure as she always did. How glad I was to see her. I caught hold of her and hugged her. She was so real and so much a part of my old life.

I can't write much and what I want to say must not be too complicated, so I'm going to let Mother do it for me.

*[Joe asked about his funeral and his mother explained]*

Joe was anxious to know what had happened since he left hospital. I told him about the cremation and that the ashes were scattered in Captain's Wood. He seemed to like that. Then I told him you'd had a memorial service at Aberford. He groaned and said, 'I suppose that was inevitable.'

Then I added, 'You have a chance to be present at the last rite, if you care to.'

'The last rite!' he exclaimed, 'but surely it's all over now.'

I told him there was still another tribute into which Douglas was to be drawn in the Guards' Chapel. He looked very puzzled and said,

'The Guards' Chapel? That was blown up in the war.'

'And rebuilt,' I added.

He seemed to think this over for some time and then said,

'If this is really true, then I suppose I ought to attend; and then laughed and added, 'I don't suppose it will matter to anyone if I'm there or not, will it?'

I said, 'Yes, it will. It may be the first link in communication between you and Lorna. Great power is generated on several planes at these services and you can have no idea how well they can be used. Anyway, if you would like to come we shall all be there with you, and Douglas has a special mention in the service so he will be taking part, and you can learn to officiate.'

This made him laugh again, 'Officiate? How extraordinary. What do you mean?'

'I mean that when you are in the etheric body and you attend one of these services, you are the natural link between the congregation (those in the physical body) and Divinity.'

This shook him and he said, 'But I couldn't do that. Douglas might, but I can't. I've never been a serious Christian, or believed in churches.'

I replied, 'Churches do hold etheric power as well as some spiritual power and both of these lines of force are now in your territory.'

He said, 'Don't make things too complicated for me or I'll lose my balance. Just tell me simply what I have to do.'

So I explained where he was to be and how he would stand between me and Douglas with Pat forming the triangle. Three is always important. I told him how he would be surrounded by our power, that he would see you all quite clearly and be able to pass quite close to Lorna, touching her aura – that is important – then passing on into the Sanctuary to stand near the altar, and that we might be slightly above the actual ground, making him feel rather tall.

*[The next day]*

This has been a most exciting re-entry into the world of matter for Joe.

The Chapel was packed with Joe's old friends from the wars, the diplomatic service and the old household. Here is a summary of what he said about it afterwards:

I'd no idea what a service could mean. I'm absolutely staggered and amazed. I floated in with you and Pat not really expecting anything and feeling rather weak. Then, as we advanced into the

102

church something happened to me. I was led irresistibly to the altar, and we stood there facing the beams of golden light which seemed to come from all the congregation, and on turning towards the altar I saw a marvellous flow of soft blue light which seemed to cover and calm me. The gold was exciting and made me feel almost back in the world, but the blue light made me think again. 'Where the devil am I and what new worlds are opening before me?' There was something in the music that seemed to be giving me an extra sense of seeing. I could see much more clearly when the choir were singing, especially at one moment when you all stood out individually right through the church. I could see everyone, not as one does in a crowd, but separately.

I want to tell you about my last visit to Chartres.

I wasn't very keen on churches, as you know. But I did know that Chartres was no ordinary church. As I walked in I met a crowd of etherics, some were coming out radiant, others were going in depressed. Some were in their sleep bodies, others were being taken by friends, having just come over in pain or some other great distress and needing special treatment.

They were all taken into the centre of the nave, where the stone circle lies, to rest and readjust themselves, before having what the helpers called 'the great experience'. Some were paralysed, some were in great mental distress. I saw the helpers straightening out their limbs, and upon them all the wonderful rays of colour fell from the rose window. To each came a different colour according to their need. The mentally disturbed ones were given green, the depressed blue and soft shades of pinks and reds; and the utterly worn out were embedded in golden rays and so on.

I suddenly realized that I knew one of the helpers, and when she turned I recognized Hilda, who had been an old friend of my youth. We were so glad to meet again, and she let me in on the technique of healing. She was mainly dealing with depression and fear. She said nearly everyone came over in this state, very, very few came willingly, that was why so many gravely ill people hung on for so long.

She had in her care an old woman, a man and a child of about ten. They were not related and she took each separately and allowed me to help. The man was old and ill and had come over in sleep, so he was an easy case; she placed him in a blue ray edged with gold to wake up slowly. The woman had been mentally disturbed, so she was given the green ray with a glorious suffusion of gold which calmed her and automatically turned into a radiant blue. The tortured features relaxed and she slept.

The child was awake and miserable and clung to Hilda, who has always had a great way with children. She too was quickly soothed and asleep.

I said 'What next?'

'Wait and see.'

But at that moment I saw another woman being brought in. She was irritable and annoyed that more was not being done for her. 'I told the Doctor,' she kept on saying, 'I knew he was wrong, I got worse and worse with those awful pills and no other treatment and now. . . .'

'Well, how do you feel now?' broke in Hilda.

'Who are you? You are not my nurse – why isn't she here? I rang my bell.'

'Yes, and then you left your body and came away with me, don't you remember?'

She looked puzzled and then said, 'Yes, of course, you came in that lovely dress of gold: it was like a ray of sunshine, and when I thought you were going to leave me I cried, and you said, 'Come with me,' and I came! Whatever made me do that?'

'Your knowledge that no healing could reach you in that place. Now we are going to heal you with rays of light, and you are going to sleep.' Turning to me she said, 'Watch.'

I saw a look of wonder come over her cross face and she relaxed into a smile and allowed herself to sink on to an etheric bench and sleep. . . .

At this moment Hilda whispered to me, 'Come into the Sanctuary. This is only the beginning. Many of those sleeping in the nave will get no further at present. They will wake up and go out into the plane of awakening, but those who are further advanced wake up and drift into the Sanctuary quite naturally. Here we have the vibrations of memory, and the development of wisdom whose vibrations can only be manipulated by very advanced people. I think you know one of them here. She is called Flo, and I will take you to her.' So she took me up to a tall, kindly looking woman and said: 'I think you must often have tried to help your cousin Joe in life.'

She turned and looked at me and I knew at once that a current of power came with her vibrations which I had experienced in rare moments of need during my past life. I was enchanted to meet her. What a woman I thought, and what a leader.

*Joe 'came with' his wife and me to Morocco and visited the ancient city of Volubilis and then on to Tangier where he had been en poste as Consul General during the last War.*

### [Patricia]

We came with you to the old Roman city. Joe was delighted. He said he remembered it all and was quite certain he'd served there in one of his lives. Quite suddenly he began to tell me about the skirmishes they'd had, and how he'd led one out from the city, and they'd got lost and ran out of water and began dying of thirst until he noticed some birds he'd seen feeding near to the city, and suggested following them at dusk to their feeding place, and the birds guided them back to safety.

After that recollection he suddenly said:

'I've been seeing the past, *my* past, and how real it was. I can feel the heat and the dry sand and the thirst. Those were days of real warfare. How we all enjoyed it. How different from France 1914–18.

'My goodness, what a place to have lived in! I like the savage strength of it all, and there is still a sense of great energy in those old walls. They were a capital lot, some of the old Legionaries. I can half remember some of their faces, and I am slowly piecing them on to faces of men I have served with in this last life. One old sergeant in the Guards stands out. He was killed on the Somme.

'Well, now to go back to Volubilis. I see that life as a wonderful easy natural life. I am not sure if I came with the Legion from Britain. I had been in Britain but that was in another life, and perhaps because of it I was put in charge of the British Legion. I was quite a chap in Volubilis! I had several other legions under me in different parts of Morocco, but it is this one particular period that I see, the others I can't see yet. It's so extraordinary remembering like this; quite suddenly I seemed to fall asleep or go into a trance and there I was in a Roman tunic and helmet, not very suitable for the desert, but I was strong and nothing mattered.

'I saw the wall I had to defend. I saw the Roman spears and my

107

own men. They were all absolutely clear and I knew their faces by heart. I couldn't have been more myself, and standing beside me was Douglas; we seem to have fought together, but he was killed in a fight, and I was inconsolable. I saw it happen just outside the walls. I saw him fall. I rushed to save him – it was too late – and from then on life was darkened until another personality came to my rescue. This was an older Captain whom I did not recognize at first in my vision, but I soon knew him to have been Lorna, a very great friend in my last life.

'He gave me confidence and a reason for living. He had suffered much and yet continued in a quiet efficient way, telling me that one must hold on to the routine of a soldier's life, and that would give me back the power and wish to continue. I came to respect him and love him dearly, and when he also fell in battle I took his place, and he seemed to be inspiring me to go on until my own turn came. We all died in battle in the end and most of us I think in Africa. I met my release somewhere near Tangier, that was why I had to go back there, but in my last life there was no call for me to penetrate further.'

It is extraordinary to come here after my experience at Volubilis with Douglas, and now to jump a couple of dozen centuries and be here with Lorna again here, and getting the news of Douglas's death. It all make a sort of jumble in my mind that I find hard to sort out. But the two remain unchanged in their reality. Douglas and Lorna. Lorna supporting and Douglas passing like a meteor through my lives and leaving me.

When I look at Tangier I see it and all the people I knew and worked with. Some are over here and I have met them, others I haven't met so far. But over it all hangs anxiety – can we ever hold out? In Britain – or in Tangier? Can I go on holding the strings with Spain? Will Spain let us down? One country after another have gone down like ninepins. *France*, my God! How I felt when I heard that France had defected! All my French blood revolted. I couldn't see France defeated, with the Maginot line just side-tracked! It was all fantastic. My mind reeled and boggled at all the 1940 disasters; and now I look back and see the brilliant flash of Dowding's defence.

By the way, I have met him again – a grand chap. In fact, we have looked at the history mould together. This is a most amazing thing to me; it seems that every event on earth casts a reflection on a sensitive belt of substance in the ether, and we can, by looking at it, calculate the effect each event had upon the rest of the era.

For instance, when I look at the frightful cataclysm in France in 1940, I see it all brilliantly illuminated by the Battle of Britain. I see the men who died in that fight continuing with their pals in the surviving planes, and carrying them to victory. It was virtually won by those who died and crashed on to the land or into the sea and bounded out of their bodies into the surviving planes. Hugh showed me all this in fits of laughter, saying *if only* I'd known this at the time. But instead I mourned for each man as though he had been my own son.

That flash seared the soul of Hitler. It was a greater, more far-reaching success than we dared to hope for in Tangier. But how it heartened us! Do you remember listening each day to the numbers of planes forced down by our chaps? I began to take hope that we might survive. But there were many long years to battle through first, but our, my Lorna, always said we should win! But you know how I trembled when I thought of England being virtually besieged. Oh, how well you stood by me in those awful days. It must have taken a lot out of you holding on for both of us. But you seem to have had a sort of pre-vision over many other things as well.

I loved Tangier fundamentally, even when it was hot and the Colony became too tiresome. We lived on each others' nerves – all this is now reflected in the ether belt.

One more thing I must tell you is about the dogs. They are reflected in the ether belt, running in and out of our lives absorbing so many disintegrating vibrations; in fact, and I tell it to you in all humility, the dogs were like mental disinfectants to the house. They always are; but during the war they outstripped themselves, and goodness knows what we should have done without them. I see now that dogs have a very special mission, and Maruka makes this plainer to me every day.

*We were both brought up on the west coast of Argyll and know Iona well – our favourite island was Scarba.   C.S.*


My next vision was of Iona. Here I became somehow in charge of the boat or boats owned by the monks. It was a very simple life and I suppose a hard life; but I was happy and secure.

I remember being sent away with a great leader through the islands. It might have been St. Columba, but I don't think so. He was able to use several rays of thought power, and I was not always necessary to him for transportation. Sometimes he seemed to use levitation entirely, but at others he came to me for help, and we sailed together. I have only broken memories of these cruises as we battled with the sea in a very small, roughly-made boat. But I know that I never feared not making harbour if he was with me, nor was there one moment's boredom with this man on board. He was gay and strong and full of laughter, and also full of interest; I knew he was expounding things which I couldn't understand then; but they stayed in my subconscious and I am gradually recalling them now.

He was always stressing that Power was deathless, and that something of great power had been created in the beginning of the world in Iona. He said we were very lucky to have made contact with this power, and it would always flow through us in the form of a magnetic current. Then as he spoke he would suddenly say, 'Ah, we've hit one now, I shall not need your help to-day,' and with that he was lifted out of the boat into the air and away towards the island of his destination, while we sailed slowly in his wake.

Cynth, this is better. I am leading the most extraordinary life. I
haven't any set residence as you might say, but I found myself
thinking with longing of Scarba – and I'm there! It's very different
on this plane and yet just the same. I find I am extremely close to
Douglas. He has made the Scarba on this plane, which seems to be
immediately above the physical island, into his earth base. He and
Father together seem to have drawn down various rays which
make one feel absolutely marvellous. After feeling ill for so long I
can't express to you what this abundance of health and strength
means to me.

As this is Douglas's earth base he is always to be found here in
some form. That is another strange development. He leaves a part
of himself here and calls it his extra body. But it need not look like
a body. It can be a burn, a rock or an animal which holds his
personality and becomes his acting self, while his greater self is
elsewhere.

I had no idea about our greater selves. Douglas has made
complete contact with his, but most of us are broken pieces; the
earth life body seems only to have held a small part of me, and
there is a much nicer Joe – in fact far too nice a Joe, who is waiting
for me, the imperfect Joe, to take over!

It's all right outside my sphere of thought and I sometimes feel
so puzzled by it all that I long to go back to the simplicity of earth
life – (even under the Labour Government!)

But those moods don't last for long. Everything is so much more
intense here. You all count so much more vitally in my life. I
began to realize in a quite terrifying way how truly and im-
measurably I was attached to Lorna. It's not only a one life
attachment, and she can't shake me off now whatever she does. I
find we have all belonged together for centuries – if such things as
centuries exist – so I have got to try and help all of you, as you
cannot avoid helping me! It's all most interesting. Pat urges me to
gather a substance which she calls 'umph'. It's a special kind of
energy which can flow between you and me and it allows me this
power to set down my thoughts and feelings and *release* an
immensity of vagueness out of my system.

112

You've no idea how refreshed and free I feel after I've written a letter through you. I can't write any more now, but let me do it again tomorrow.

This is my attempt to explain to you something of the vast extent of your planet of which you and all mankind have no idea – the Sea.

We were a party, Pat, Douglas, Olga, Arthur and Richard *[my brother-in-law. C.S.]*. Some had already been part of the way before, but we were intending to go further.

Armed with our knowledge of some of the higher worlds and the wonderful escape route of Chartres we entered the sea from Iona and followed the coast line, sinking slowly because of the innumerable caverns lighted now by our own etheric light, and by the thousand rays that each separate vibration emits from its own personal wave length.

I must pause here and explain your blindness! Light exists everywhere and at all times, but you couldn't live with the intense light that surrounds you. Every single thing in this room is emitting sound and light, your blankets, the pillows, the carpet: but what a jazzed-up world it would be if you could see and hear it all! Your houses would be much simpler and have far less conflicting furniture inside them.

But to go back to the sea. We can open or close the ability to see and hear, and so we proceeded with full consciousness.

The under world of the sea around our west coast islands is absolutely entrancing. It is Fairyland – untouched by the desecration of man. I could have lingered there forever but the others pressed on. As we left the surface, life became more of the snake-like variety. We do not register cold but I could see its effects upon the marine vegetation. Other strange lights began to glow over certain places and these we found to be holes or tunnels leading down into the earth or the ocean. This was again a radiance quite different from earth; and a cadence of sound or music which I cannot define seemed to have a mesmeric power, not one which dulled our senses but sharpened them.

I followed with the rest down the tunnel which seemed to be lined with gold; the light issuing from it was dazzling. On and on it led until I was beginning to wonder if we should soon arrive in New Zealand! Then the light changed and there seemed to be a rush of air bringing the scent of flowers and trees. It felt almost earthly and we emerged from our tunnel on to a promontory of radiance which is quite indescribable. I turned to Arthur – he had penetrated this way before and was accustomed to the change. Suddenly we met other beings like ourselves who were exploring, and others who had made the journey long ago and had found this strange oasis of light and used it for the development of other senses.

I can't tell you how exciting it was and how I strained every nerve to absorb and understand all around me, which I couldn't possibly have done without this strange mesmeric vibration which seemed to be keeping me on my toes all the time.

We were led into a big circle of people, some of whom I began to recognize from other lives, and with a sudden burst of recognition I saw the monk from Iona, whose boatman I had been long ago. I *knew* it was the same man, but grown even more dynamic and very far advanced and now to me even god-like.

I seized his hand and we reclaimed each other. It was the strangest moment. Had I not been kept sane by the presence of Pat and Douglas I think I should have dissolved into nothingness! That is the feeling these experiences give one – that one is sloughing off more and more of the useless bits of one's personality – with an awful dread, that soon there may be *nothing* left. But Pat and Douglas just laugh at my fears.

115

I should like to finish my description of my first undersea journey.
I left you on the Promontory of Light, where the old monks from
Iona had made a centre, or from where I should say the Ionic
power originally stemmed. I was told, having been shown the
power centres on the surface of the earth, that I was now going to
be shown where they came from and how they emerged.

We all knew that the power from Iona dated from pre-historic
times and that the monks were led to gather and protect it, but
how did it first originate?

Leaving our oasis of light we passed into an atmosphere of
blueness very like the earth sky. Neither water nor land appear
solid to us. We can pass through all natural substances, and I was
told we were actually passing through the so-called solid earth. In
the beginning when the planets of our own solar system were
created, a vast explosion of divine force was allowed to enter the
nebulae, and working from the very centre of each and every cloud
of this gaseous element, the force began to circulate and by doing
so in a circular method, started the first element of movement and
growth and power; and as the worlds became ready to support life,
the motion system continued throughout all creation: the flow of
the tides and seasons.

The flow of the blood was then created as the bearer of the
divine current of life; and so into every living, moving entity,
movement became life in all its different rhythms.

We were being shown as much as we could accept, and I began
to wonder if my power of acceptance was equal to the task.

This complete loss of the tangible feeling of earth, which was
now to me no more than an extended sky, was cutting the ground
from beneath my feet with a vengeance. I said this to Douglas, and
he laughed and replied, 'Hold on to the thought of the physical
being real, this is only another form of it and we don't want you to
lose touch with earth for a long time yet, you are such a good link
on paper!' So, feeling the warmth from all this praise, I kept on
saying to myself, 'Only earth in another form – water turned to
vapour,' and we moved on.

Sometimes we passed through beams of light obviously making

for the earth surface centre; these became more and more frequent until I became aware of a new sense altogether. I can't describe it; there was a deep thunderous roar, which, though thunderous was never deafening: it was more like some gigantic heart beating and throbbing in such a personal way that each one of us seemed to respond as though we had ceased to be separate individuals and were instead all linked up with the vast throbbing force.

Instead of feeling unable to absorb any more, I felt refreshed and strong, as though I was being filled with energy like the blowing up of a balloon! I was growing larger, at least I felt like it. I looked at Pat and Douglas to see if they had changed, and I had the same odd sensation which came to me at Christmas when they took me into the upper ether and we all became invisible to each other. Here it was again, this great Christ Power surging through us, making and remaking every cell in our crystal-clear bodies.

This, I was told, was the centre of the earth, the power house from which all life has sprung and towards this all physical life must return.

Well, we all grow slowly, but you know death does change us all very considerably. It's the complete freedom. No money to worry over, no health problem, no possessions – because we possess all. Perhaps employment, or the lack of it is the most severe test. I felt the loss of my job on earth very acutely, and could never settle into anything else. Here I found the constant excitement and the newness and awareness of our new abilities took my breath away, and constant short assignments kept me on my toes, but continuity does not appear to exist. it's a continual change. Perhaps Flo can tell you how she can keep the even tenor of her healing ray, but I think even that fluctuates. This is one of the new conditions of life.

Those who come over after or during a long life of routine first feel a great release and then a great blank. I was asked to go and help some of our own office staff. I'd known some of them and they were full of the joys of living, but they all said, 'What do we *do*? It's like a long holiday, but that's not enough.' So I suggested travel, and why not visit the coasts and go under water like your sister-in-law, Dorothy. One man did this and came back full of excitement. He'd made contact with sharks and whales and found they were excellent company and not at all anti-man as he expected, but equally full of curiosity about us and very anxious to explore our world. So he brought a few whales and dolphins into our upper ether, and I had quite a long chat with them while they wriggled about in our atmosphere appearing to be equally comfortable among the etheric currents. They have very clear thought patterns which I am learning to sense. Your Arthur is an expert in thought patterns and he taught me how to sort them out.

The whales were delighted to be welcomed by Man, and said they had been excluded from human contact for centuries and centuries, and now at last the time had come when they could enter the ether and merge their great powers with ours. This fascinated me, they were so big and so radiant. They have a different wave length from ours and a tremendous power for both sending out and absorbing the rays.

In the end our development either here or with you depends

entirely upon our power to *give* and *take*. Do you remember the old tag? Are you radio-active? Well, that is just what the whales are.

I'd never gone very far under the sea though I'd explored Corrikrecken, but I wasn't taking in all the complex elements at that time. Now I find this hierachy of sea life has gone a long way beyond us in the thinking line. It's hard work doing a piece of plain thinking in our old physical atmosphere; the air does not receive and send on thought waves nearly as easily as the water. Marconi discovered this when he entered the water in his etheric state. He said, 'Now I can listen backwards and forwards. I can hear the Sermon on the Mount or its equivalent as expressed in the sea, and I can listen forward to the words of the Great Christ speaking to those advanced enough to understand.'

There is another overwhelming sense of the presence of Christ in the water. I am on the edge of discovering this faculty and tomorrow I should like to tell you about my first big journey under water.

# PLANTS, SAILING, IONA,
## DOROTHY AND HER SEA CREATURES

I long to try and give you a picture of life over here. Lorna accepts all I write, but she still can't think of me as really living. I want her to know that I am around, that my days, (and no nights) are divided into periods when I am with her at H.L. or in the mind world of her making – I mean her thinking. We all create a mind world to which we retreat and in which we have a real feeling of life. Lorna's is among animals; she gives and receives through the animal and the plant world; people drain her and she gains nothing from them, so we must help the animal plant channel to grow.

All animals, birds, and plants have what I can only call looser auras. They are continually sympathetic; they give out all the time, and they hardly seem to need to take in at all. Now the human animal has got itself into a corner, he has forced his aura tightly into his body, so, generally speaking, he is not sympathetic to all and sundry. He gives when he wants to, and withdraws most of the time. Man was constructed to be the main Giver in life, the day was meant for giving, and the night for drawing in the extended power of the Creator. Lorna is naturally a good sleeper which, as you know, I never was. So urge her to think of me or of animals or plants on going to sleep. This will bring refreshment and, I hope, healing to the body. (I'm becoming a really prosy old sermonizer!)

But I want you both to know how it works. I get drained too and have to go and cook up some more energy, and this I do either in the Jag or in the Bluebell. D. and I make a great thing of the Bluebell. Do you remember how hampered we used to be by time, weather and wind! Now it's all quite different; the weather and the breeze are for us to command, and the sailing is as simple as driving a Jag. We've explored the coast, the islands, the caves, and the whirlpools as we never could before, and I've learnt a whole lot about Iona and Holy Isle, and the waiting forces that are all there. St. Columba was the interpreter. He brought them to the surface. You know, Cynth, we've been lucky to have been brought up at Craignish with all this flowing through our auras in child-hood; I wasn't nearly so open to it as you were, but it was there. And now I can tap it all and join in with you and Mother and

120

Douglas. Lorna sensed it too but for so short a time; I wish you could take her to Iona – perhaps one day.

All this lovely coast has an immense future. At the moment it is only glimpsed by those in the body, but teeming numbers of etherics go there all the time. Luckily they are not like a packaged tour befouling the whole place; but they are only the ones who are awake to this particular power.

Until quite lately only the Christian initiates have been using it, but now I meet all kinds of Easterners merging their rays with the old Iona power. When I say *old* that is only relative, the saints are as up to the minute as they can be. Such a delightful group. They *are* magnetic, and they hold their groups and teach, quite uninterrupted by the physical life that worries on around.

I have been able to pass from the seeing and hearing, the physical to the etheric; and they tell me there are many entirely different circles of life going on all the time on other vibs, quite unconscious and completely insulated from the rest. All this is quite new to me and I find it enthralling. When I have had enough, or taken in all I can, we plunge into the sea and explore the caves and sea creatures physical and etheric; and here I meet your sister-in-law, Dorothy. She is one of the great sea initiates, she *is* a forward looking woman! I've heard all about the etheric home for naughty girls at Gweedore! She seems to be growing on some of my lines, we had some good laughs together. She has a great intimacy with the whales and dolphins, or the porpoises of our waters. Dorothy talks gaily to them in or out of the body. They seem to be completely ambi-plane if there is such a word, and Dorothy loves them all and is content to spend very long periods among them. I can't do that, I want change, I want to move from one plane of thought to another; with all this multiplicity of life around me I just can't wait to see more.

*This is perhaps the place to insert letters about, and from Pat's Aunt Dot, who had lived a frustrated life on earth. Finding she could produce a dream house, she used it for the reception of all kinds of people, some advanced and others less so, who found themselves suddenly on the next plane. Subsequently she entered the sea and made contact with all sea creatures.*

[Patricia] Dot's home is only partly illusion. She is very near the physical ether which means it is attainable for people without much development who come over with their earth desires unsatisfied, and in the ether of Dot's home, are able to construct just those same satisfying conditions which she had lacked throughout her own earth life. So the Tarts' home is *wonderful*!

You walk from one illusion to another. Some saw themselves as running a casino, others a theatre or concert hall; to all of them self-expression with the appearance of success was produced on the ether. This is, of course, illusion, because it is only the desire of the ego for success and fame. We all need some measure of satisfaction. So Dot's home for these super-extroverts is very colourful, but not without value; for instance, I heard the rippling sound of a piano being beautifully played and a wonderful voice launching itself into a riot of song. Egotistic? Yes, of course, but a stepping stone to the music spheres.

The line of demarcation between the purely egotistic, and the desire to allow the universal music to flow through is very close indeed, and many cross the border under Dot's care.

Dot came here to fulfil her earth desires, and they have been long since completely quenched, but she continues to help all those who in like disposition came over with what she calls a 'hot fury' under their skin! Dot is doing a wonderful job, and it is all her own; but having exhausted her egocentric desires, she has called on many of the family and all kinds of more advanced people to help.

As I told you she has now a side-line, an Aqua Home for all kinds of fish life which have been slaughtered by man, and allowed to suffer. The slaying is accepted, but the causation of suffering is *not*. So we have whales and cod and all kinds of fish resting in a

123

calming atmosphere before reincarnating! Dot adores them, it's a 'thing' with her. She wanders among the big whales soothing them and crooning to them. She has awakened quite a new vib in herself and in all of us who come to join her.

You ask about Lady B., who floated off when the Tarts arrived. Well, she came back! She missed the home-like atmosphere and on returning found Dot at the bottom of her etheric bay, working on the whales! Lady B. was horrified and terrified and quite speechless! Dot, who had always seemed to her to be a perfectly normal person was patting and crooning softly to a small gathering of surly looking whales and sharks! To her great credit, Lady B. stood her ground and waited. Someone reminded her that there was no physical danger, and after a few minutes the audience became less surly, tail flailing ceased, and Dot continued with her rhythmic crooning, which seemed to pacify them, until these great hulking brutes began a queer hissing sound which deepened in tone and became a sort of deep accompaniment to Dot's treble notes! It was fascinating to watch. Directly she had gained this stage of relaxation she turned it into a ray note and left her new patients under its influence, while she turned to welcome Lady B. 'My dear, how nice to see you,' were her first words; and Lady B. not expecting such a welcome suddenly thawed out, partly the result of her recent terror, and partly through the delight of Dot's welcome. She suddenly asked Dot if she could use her in any way for her work? Dot was delighted and said what kind of work? 'Oh, anything, I'm so tired of doing nothing.' So now she is one of the staff!

Dot keeps the whole place going, gardens, library, dining room, cocktail bar, etc., so there is plenty of work repairing and rethinking all these sides of life. Lady B. is now doing the gardens and the library, with frequent dives into the piscatorium or whatever they call it. I often go for a laugh and a rest. It's all so gay and happy.

Dot is preparing to go further and work for animals too, but that is being done by many people while fish life has been rather overlooked.

Dot says she works for the 'castaways'! But you'd hardly agree if you could look in upon some of her very highly-coloured ladies and their swains! The swain part is very typical. They are drawn here by the desire for sex, thinking that anyway they are not cut off from some of the joys of living, as they'd known them. They find a willing tart and proceed as before – but they have no sex organs! So what? Something quite different. Through lying together the auras become enmeshed. As you know, a man's rotates one way and a woman's the other, so once they are in contact with a definite thought link, they suddenly find a curious feeling of at-oneness coming over them, (you and Pa have experienced this in mutual prayer), and of course over here it is far stronger. They feel drawn together as by a magnet, it exhilarates and unites and they become lovers in a higher sense which of course they don't understand, but are quite ready to enjoy. This continues until an urge grows in them to go further. They have mixed with the rest in the dining room and the cocktail bar and they have all danced together: in this way they fulfil the lust instincts, and often leave in couples to explore, to travel and sometimes to work for some bigger cause allowing Universal Spirit to flow through them.

My love
Tricia


*[Dot herself continues her story]*

I want to tell you about my life among the sea creatures. I began my new life at Gweedore, and eventually followed it on to the shore and fell in love with sea life. I was allowed to enter solid rock which I no longer found solid, and so I became almost at one with the earth vib – but still I returned to the sea and worked with the sea creatures. I explored the oceans and learnt from them the sea lore and the history or legends of the incarnation of Christ among the sea creatures. He came among men as a man, he came among the sea creatures as one of themselves.

He overlighted first the whale and then the dolphin, the seal and so on through the greater and lesser forms of sea life; and they accepted him and withdrew to formulate their own ways of advancement.

I was horrified at first that our Christ should have entered the spirit body of a sea monster! But I soon accepted it. They communicated all this to me, sometimes by sound, but more often

125

by the movement of their pricelessly flexible bodies. Movement is the medium of sea talk. I began to learn it and to enter into their delightful sense of flexibility, taking from them the sheer joy of movement. 'That is Christ-given,' they told me. 'Our movement and your laughter are one and the same vibration.' This gave me pause for thought, and I lived among these strange creatures, loving them and they loving me, with an amazingly unpossessive love which was quite beautiful.

One day I noticed the most glorious light shining in the depths. I thought at first that it was the blue light from earth, but I very soon realized it was the Christ presence among the sea folk: the moment in time when Christ enters the water and revitalizes it with his flaming presence.

Then everything began to glisten, and the sea itself danced with its teeming mass of myriad types of life – and all life worshipped him.

# CHRISTMAS AND THE ENJOYMENT GLAND

*[Joe]*

This is a good moment for telling you my news. I've been Christmassing in quite a different way. I always thought it was rather pointless the way we ate and drank and gave parties, and some went to church to sing carols about things they knew and cared nothing about. It was all so silly.

Now, I've had a peep behind the scenes and what a Christmas we have over here. No feasting and drinking, well, I don't mind that. I was afraid I'd be asked to think deeply and do all kinds of mental work, but no – I was just told to *watch* and see what I could, and enjoy it. That was the big purpose, open yourself to *enjoy* everything. There seems to be an organ in this etheric body which they call the enjoyment gland. They say we all had it on earth, but a great many people let it wither away from lack of use, and I certainly knew a few in that category. But, although mine was not well developed, it was still there, and I knew how to enjoy certain things; my new organ can enjoy almost anything, and exponents of this faculty volunteer to go back to the material plane and the lower etheric planes and lend enjoyment to the simpler forms of life.

Douglas told me he always did this at Christmas and would I like to go with him. Of course it was much more my line than sailing up into the ether and lodging temporarily among the more advanced. I loved the old earth, so I was given some training on how to approach those in the body, and off we went. Douglas, as you know, is very keen on music, so it was through the music vib that we came into touch with earth. Carols, *Good King Wenceslas* and all that. I laughed to find it all going on as usual, and I enjoyed it, my gland was working well! We went into several houses with children who were whooping it up properly, and then on to a pub where a lot of people were trying to comfort themselves with a *lot* of whisky!

Here I met for the first time a number of the simpler etherics, whom Douglas has worked with. They were not actually alcoholics, but they still found most of their pleasure in swigging down whisky. This all seemed very natural to me, and yet rather pointless. They weren't getting any real enjoyment. I tried to give

127

them the feeling I used to have, but it seemed very unsatisfying, and I was losing touch all round. I looked for Douglas who was laughing away with a group of etherics, telling them they'd better pack it all in and come and try some of our vintages. One of them said, 'All right. Let's go.' The man looked a hardened old soaker, but he'd come to the end, and he turned on me as a newcomer and said, 'It's bad stuff here. Nothing worth tasting. Have a drink?'

I took the glass he offered and tried to drink it. It looked all right, but during the last months I have lost all taste for it, so it was strange to me and tasted sour.

Douglas whispered, 'It's not your liquor, Daddy, any longer, don't touch it.' But one had to accept a drink. In a moment I began to feel fuddled and awful. There was something in the drink that burnt me.

'Enjoy it,' said Douglas. I made a great effort to do so and recovered instantly. Was this the key to depression?

I looked round and found an old man, an etheric, but still old. So I went up to him and said, 'Having a good time?'

He shook his head. 'Nothing any good now,' he said wearily. I began working my new gland on him and he relaxed.

'Well, I suppose it's not so bad really, but one was led to expect more than this.'

'What did you expect?' I asked.

'Oh, well, I suppose I expected a Heaven of some sort; but this was all I found.'

'Did you really believe in Heaven?' said Douglas breezily.

'Well, no. I thought it was all my eye, but something has to happen, doesn't it?'

'Well, it depends on you. Have you had enough of this? Would you like to see a little more of Heaven?'

'Yes,' he replied, 'but I haven't seen anything yet.'

'Come with us and we'll show you something more.'

He came, rather unwillingly, and Douglas saw that the man had worked with machines in a factory and took him to the area where the thought creation takes form. He looked mystified and asked what it was all about.

'It's your old factory on this plane. I thought you'd like to see the production level here.'

'But where are all the benches and machine tools?'

'They are in your mind – no need to turn screws and nuts. Here you do it by thought, and the contrivance for speed travel becomes a ray of moving light.'

'It's what I used to see when a train passed quickly in the twilight.'

'Yes, that is just the moment you see both sides.'

Suddenly all sense of disappointment and depression fell away from him and he became as interested and as young as I was feeling myself.

I was rather empty, I'd given all I had by this time and D. told me to go back to my own plane and think this over. It certainly had given me a lot of food for thought.

*This was another 'looking back' letter when Joe saw himself again with Douglas, his only son in his last life, who was killed in France in 1944.*

My life in France in the Middle Ages seems to have begun in the north where war and famine and misery and a general chaotic state prevailed. It was all so disorganized that in course of time I seemed to drift south.

I remember my meeting with Douglas. I was alone and very thirsty – my men had gone off to their homes to plough the land to try to raise food for their families. I was drifting. Douglas passed me and we looked at each other. I can see him now in the neat simple robe of a clerk, while I was dirty and in rags. Something urged him to invite me into his house for food and wine. I accepted readily and we went together to a small mud and stone house, very simple, just what an artist would need. 'This is part of the Monastery,' he explained, as he offered me bread and wine. That was the beginning of one of the happiest periods of all my memories. I am going to try and track the Monastery. It was among olive groves and within sight of the sea.

Douglas was living on the artistic plane where music, painting and prayer were all woven inextricably together.

It was in a sense a very perfect life of utter simplicity. I can't remember any household chores. We ate and slept when we were hungry or needed rest. Food of some sort was available – fruit, bread, wine, I think that was all we had, probably mostly from the Monastery, but it was all very primitive and must have been a very small settlement. Douglas seemed hardly to belong to this world, and I don't know how or when he passed over. But there appeared to be very little difference in our lives. He was there working as before. The music was there, the painting continued, our conversations were uninterrupted – the only thing I noticed was that he had ceased to eat and seemed not to need food or wine. I thought this odd and unnatural but he assured me that many of the Brothers were like him now and found they needed very little rest and no food. So I accepted his queer ways, since he had always been an eccentric to my way of thinking.

Then I began to notice a certain radiance around him. He was always lightly made or rather spare of form, not heavy like me.

One evening I came in from the night when it was quite dark and found him painting with a light issuing entirely from his own body. I can see it so plainly, and my consternation. 'Douglas! What are you doing and where is the light coming from?'

'Me,' he said quite simply. 'Don't you understand, I've let go my physical body and am using the next one.'

'But where is your old body of flesh and blood?'

It's not here any longer, it's gone into the ether. The Brothers showed me how to do this. I'm just the same now only I work better and my work has lasting quality,'

'But then you are – dead!' I said in astonishment.

Whereupon he roared with laughter, 'Not dead at all but very much more alive than I ever was. It's quite wonderful. I feel so strong and untiring. I can *do* things now. I carried a painting into the Infirmary today and put it beside a dying man. He shot up on his bed as he saw the 'Shining One' and fell back as happy as a child to pass over without fear.

'I'm hearing all kinds of things and "seeing"! I'll tell you more gradually each day, but go and get your meal now and rest; don't worry about me. I'm stronger than both of us put together.'

I had a long drink of wine after that to steady my nerves – to try to think out what he meant! I've run out of power, but you see this old life is *very* important to me. I *must* remember it and see how vital Douglas has been to me in life after life.

I do not know how long he was able to continue in this state. It depends on the desire. With Douglas it continued until I was ready to pass on. We lived together so far as I can remember in the same way – Douglas doing more painting and music and spending longer intervals in the Infirmary to heal and teach. And then when I became ill, and I knew my strength was ebbing fast, Douglas came and told me he was going to help me to leave the physical aching body and reassume for a time the same body as he was using.

I fell into a coma, and woke to find myself outside my body, which was lying most awkwardly across a rough bed. Douglas was there; he did not attempt to move or straighten the corpse; he just stood, and I knew he was deep in prayer, asking the Great Powers of Earth to receive my old body. Then, turning to me, he said,

'Come outside, you must need air and sunshine,' and we moved into the little olive garden outside. I breathed deeply the most wonderful air. Something entered into me with that breathing and gave me another sense.

When we returned to the hut, my old body had vanished and Douglas was saying, 'We shall not see it again. The earth is ours and all that is in it.'

And so I began my astral semi-physical life for a short time with Douglas, but I was not far enough advanced by a long chalk and so after a period – I don't know how long – I lost touch with my astral and became etheric, leaving Douglas to continue his work among the poor and suffering, painting and writing music and remaining between the planes; while I in my unevolved etheric flowed back into the usual stream of life and rest after physical death. In other words, I ceased to be useful on the semi-physical plane.

I am told there are many advanced souls who are enabled to do this, particularly in times of stress.

Now to go back to our journey into the earth. We reached the centre, at least I suppose we did, and having exhausted our power to accept new vibrations we turned for the surface, coming back slowly, endeavouring to see all we could.

The earth has a very thick crust, which is very off-putting on first acquaintance, and Mary found it suffocating: it feels like passing through thick pea soup, but it doesn't last. The earth has enormous caverns, lighted by a different kind of light from anything I had seen before on the surface or in space. This is due, I'm told, to a mixture of sun and moon rays passing through the soil. I can't describe it, it's quite 'unearthly' as we used to say, but most beautiful and ringing with music.

I asked Andrew what the sound meant, and he said they are calling into life the new seeds and buds that will later grow and flourish on the surface. I couldn't see the roof of the cavern that we passed through, it was immense. When I looked up I saw only a haze of light.

There were beings everywhere, large and small nature spirits and Devas, and another line altogether living in clusters among fairy-like gossamer webs, hanging and swaying with no apparent effort and with no support. But gravitation works quite differently here, and in any case we do not seem to notice it; but we do feel an impelling attraction towards the centre, and I was sad to turn away.

Flo, as usual the practical Flo, said, 'We've learnt all we can on this venture, let's go back to our "thinking places" and sort out what we have gained.'

Our 'thinking places' are wherever we made our etheric base. Mine, like Douglas's, is within hail of Scarba and Corrikrecken. The earth caverns had a cousinly feeling to those below the whirl pool and Iona, where we met the old monks on the Promontory. This was all on the same set of vibrations.

I dallied and let Flo slip off home, while R. and I followed slowly. She had never penetrated into so many different types of vib, and her power of acceptance is growing rapidly. 'I must find out about this music, Joe.' So off she went into the upper reaches of the cavern, following the strains and asking for guidance. She came back radiant with excitement, saying, 'Oh Joe, I've met some of the old Masters. They are trying out new sounds and learning how they were able to produce the music which came to them on earth. It's all founded and grounded here, (if anything is grounded).' She added, 'But they tell me nothing really originated from here, it came upon some type of wireless ray which carries sound inspiration from sun to star, so it all comes from the sun or suns, and we don't really know where any of our wonderful recordings came from, and they are all *recordings!*'

She went on to tell me that Bach was here and Mozart and many others, that is, a part of them, or one of their auxiliary bodies.

At this point I urged her to come home, telling her that I couldn't carry any more new ideas.

And so we left the Great Cavern, and entered the pea soup crust, and came back to the daylight that we knew and loved.

Cynth, I am changing a lot. I don't really know myself now as the old class-conscious diplomat! I was, you know! I used to find it very hard really to like people outside my own set. Now I've shed all that like a chrysalis, and can stand outside it and wonder that it had ever had such a power to sway me. In a way perhaps it does still!

I've just been looking into the lives of the miners. My God, I am glad I wasn't called upon to work in the pits. We never thought much of it; we used to go down now and then, and it seemed to compare quite well with the land worker, but now I'm not so sure. There is something so deadly about working underground, and perhaps being crushed to death and suffocated. I think you'll have to find a substitute for coal. Gas has been given you from the North Sea. This I did not realize was growing so extensive, and so very strong, far too strong for the old gas system. I'm told you'll go on finding more, but the problem remains.

I've met some of the scientists who are looking for a lead on how to split the atom without coal. Of course I'm no scientist, but Douglas (Douglas G.)* always old Douglas to us, now looks as young and gay as any young Guardsman. He offered to take me to the Moon to see how they are working out new methods in an undisturbed atmosphere. I was all for it, but I wondered if I was quite ready for such a party! I asked Pat, and she said, 'Yes but, you'll need two people, one of each side. Have you been into the upper ether?'

I said 'No, not above Everest.'

'Come on then, we'll take you now and you can see just what it feels like.'

So I was told how to accustom myself to height, and withdraw all the physical ether from my etheric body. I found this tedious and exhausting, and not very pleasant. I liked my physical vibs and I wanted to hold on to them. They gave me access to you and Lorna, and I seemed to be separating myself completely. Pat assured me that this was not so, and after a long trial for readjustment we took off, Pat and Douglas in attendance. Yes, I was well off the ground

* Sir Douglas Galton, Joe's and C.'s grandfather.

and we seemed to be passing through layers of coloured fog. It wasn't unpleasant, but I felt they were taking me right outside all that was remotely familiar, and I was a bit scared! I seemed to be growing less and less the personal *me*. They sensed this but they only laughed. Pat told me she had felt the earth pull very keenly, but once broken one was free to go and return. I wasn't at all sure that I wanted to go at all, and reminded her that I had Lorna to think of, and wouldn't it be better to wait until she came over? 'Well, it's up to you,' was their reply, 'but you won't be any further from Lorna. Love brings all things and people into close touch.'

I wanted to say 'Well, I can't accept that,' but I felt like clay in their hands, and so we went on.

From being fabulously light I became terribly heavy, and I saw they were actually having to lift me. 'Don't worry,' they both said, 'You are nearing the point where gravitation becomes orbital, and once past that point you are free.'

I felt awful, so heavy and stupid – and then suddenly it all ceased and I was light again and rushing through the ether in clear view of both earth and moon.

This was such a contrast, to find myself again, that I became wildly happy. . . . Can't write any more today.

\*　　　\*　　　\*

Now I want to go back to my trip to the moon. Once outside the orbital pull of the earth I was *free*, and what excited me among other things was that we were not in darkness, as I had imagined. That is what one experienced by the physical eye which cannot take in these other rays of superb light. This is *real light*. That was my first exciting discovery. Light becomes an element with texture that laps round one. I felt myself going out towards this light, embracing it with all my delight and human welcome for something so utterly outside my experience, and yet something which responded to a built-in longing deep inside me. I know this all sound very extravagant, and not at all me, but it is, Lorny – I'm changing, I can't help it, I don't want to help it. It's magical and beautiful and beyond all words to describe. In the wonder and beauty of space we find complete *freedom*.

I had no desire to move out of the element, but I was drawn on into the orbital magnetic currents of the moon. Not the moon as we saw it from the astronauts' photographs, perhaps something remotely resembling it, but infinitely more lovely. Instead of the hard, cold desert landscape here was something covered with a gossamer texture of many colours What had been seen physically might have been the skeleton of a dead world, while we were being shown the body of flesh covering, etheric and complete.

I cannot write any more today.

*　　　*　　　*

I want to go on and tell you about the moon. It's so fantastic; it's like beginning all over again. It's another way of living, thinking and being against quite a different vibration from earth; and yet we do belong to the moon in some subtle sense which I cannot define.

The whole scene is so different. Vegetation? Yes, but of quite a different kind. Whereas on earth we see your material vegetation plus the etheric counterpart, here there is no material vegetation at all. It is as though the whole sphere had been cleared for the use of our plane, with only this backbone of stark physical matter to form the link.

We stood on a soft moss-like substance, and colour was every-where. At first I saw no one. Then I began to notice many people of different races. Pat told me they were mostly scientists, and that we should find Douglas Galton and probably your Arthur here. I waited, trying to accustom myself to these strange vibrations. Pat and Douglas meanwhile were changing under my eye; they were full of force and energy and obviously these different elements.

I asked Pat to explain the position, to which she replied quite calmly, 'We belong here more completely than we do to earth, so coming here is like coming home to our own vibrations. You have still so many physical vibs that you can't understand how much we love the moon, and have grown into friendship with all this form of life and vegetation. Just look at our forests! They are quite different from those on earth but they are tree-conscious. That means the great tree spirits of earth live here and reflect their power towards the earth forests, giving them the forces which they need, and which are now being cut off from earth owing to man's pollution of the planet.'

At this moment Douglas came and joined us. He looked so young, while I was still feeling rather 'earth-worn', (that is the expression used here, before becoming a full etheric).

Douglas gave me a splendid welcome. 'Gwendolen's son, I am glad to have you here at last. How receptive do you feel?' I thought, what an awkward question! I didn't feel in the least receptive. I was feeling completely strange and out of contact. He took my hand, and as though reading my thoughts, said, 'This will leave you and you will begin to see with our eyes and hear with our ears. Now, to explain: many of us here are working upon the methods for speeding up etheric development on earth. Here we can work without the hindering, delaying vibrations of earthly discord. We need people like you to advise and show us how our suggested treatments will react. Do you mind being a guinea-pig?'

I was delighted to find a niche, since I had been feeling so completely out of touch that any way in which I could help would bring me closer to this strange world.

They took me into what they called the forest. We brushed past living branches that were more like beautiful humanesque limbs covered in leafy stuff of all colours: quite different from earth and quite indescribable.

'Now,' said Douglas, as we dropped lightly into a clearing, 'I want you to imagine you are back in the earth body. We can help you to feel the old sensations.'

After a few moments I did feel this and it frightened me! It was hateful to take on again the earth sensation of weight and I shuddered with the horror and discomfort of it.

'Now,' said Douglas, 'we want you of your own volition to drop this feeling of weight. Know yourself to be a creature of *light*.'

As he said this I began to regain my hard-won sense of weightlessness, and how glad I was. I lifted myself off the surface and began to feel at one with the forms around me.

'Good,' said D.G., 'I am glad you've come. You'll be able to help us a great deal if you are willing to, and then go back to earth and try to teach those in the physical how they can shed their coarser vibrations here and now, without experiencing the awful period of old age and decrepitude.'

I was delighted as I thought of you all, and was filled with the desire to learn and help.

Then D.G. left me and Douglas and Pat said that this was enough for one experience, and they would take me back to earth to recover from the shock and to absorb all I'd learnt, and restock with earth vibs for my further experiments.

So, Lorny dear, this is a great step in my new life. I don't feel quite equal to it, but when I said this to D. he only laughed. 'We all feel that at the start, but power is universal, and there is no lack of ability, only the limitation we put upon our acceptance of it.'

I don't think I've given you one tiny glimpse of the wealth and scope of this experience, but there I must leave it. With all my love and hopes of being able to express this great system of evolution more clearly.

*       *       *

Cynth, so our writing sessions are over for a time. When we next write I shall hope to have learnt more about development. In the mean time do try *all* of you, especially you Cynth and Lorna to *see* yourselves as beings of *light*. In this way you will draw the light elements into your physical body, and prepare for the change over from physical to etheric. Take a few moments each day, preferably just as you wake and before you go to sleep, but any time of the day when you are waiting for someone or something. Sit still and draw *light* into your lungs and heart and brain – just light. After you have done this several times you may begin to feel the physical is less heavy to move. Douglas says this is very important and could be the start for the sense of weightlessness which we all yearn for as we grow old and heavy in the physical body. I remember it all so well.

I was shown briefly some of the areas set aside for the recovery of earth – as they call it! Ways for destroying pollution and recultivating the earth. These are the plans to give earth a new vibration. You are running out of the present vib, that is your trouble, as well as all the elements that go with it. So another vib or set of vibs is being prepared to take over on earth. This will be quite a new method of living, thinking and believing. The leader in all this is the Christ.

I was taken to the edge of what was called the super Christed area, where the Christed ones were working to produce and reflect these new powers upon earth. All of us are to become the bearers of this power (if I can prove myself able for the task; Pat and Douglas have been doing this already). We shall be used as emissaries between earth and moon. It's a most exciting venture for me, and quite in line with all I learnt in my earth life. So you see, Lorny dear, diplomacy goes on, and on . . .! Now it's not trade or political relations, but the importation of *light*.

One last word. Please learn to live more with the moon! When the sky is clear *look* at the moon, and at night draw consciously from that pale, lovely light which you will soon begin to identify as a subtle vibration of its own. Let it enter your earth body and draw in a deep breath and send it consciously all over your body, lungs, heart and brain. I will give you other centres of power later. Just try to absorb moon power into these three organs.

Your growing and not doubting

Joe

140

Cynth, I am waiting to tell you about the etheric belt. This is exciting.

I told you we used the vibs from the soil for cultivation, but that a tiny percentage was of a different vib. It seemed to come from the very soul of the earth; it came to us as a gentle questing breath from another world, passing through the soil and the people working on it and going on – into infinity. What was this new vib, what was it searching for? Everest? Chartres? No, that was not its goal. I refrained from going further until I was given the directive to draw the vib into my aura and to transport it into the upper ether – the stratosphere.

I had been into this region before with Douglas and Pat, but never alone. I called for help, but I was told to 'go it alone'. This I found difficult. It was so hard to leave the gravitational pull of earth. I had asked for the power of Everest and Chartres, and together the currents bore me up out of the gravitational pull of earth until I reached the orbital circle. Was this far enough? For the moment, yes. But I must go further, this orbital circle was a resting station. It was calm and quiet and completely harmonious. I felt I wanted to stay there indefinitely, but the vibrations I was bearing in my aura from earth were pricking me to go on. Around me was a sensitive belt of colour, I was breathing this into my finer body and asking to be led through it to a finer belt of vibration where I could unload my earth vibs, and go home! But for a time I was held in the balance, not knowing what to do, and alone in space. Fear, as we used to know it, had completely left me, but the longing for the now familiar way of life was pressing me to end this mission.

Suddenly into my aloneness came a voice telling me that the next stage of my journey was not through space but into space. I had to accept the inner calm, and search within for a further layer of thinking that would satisfy the earth vibs, and allow them to find their own level. So, speaking to the earth vib as though it were my child, I said, 'Where shall we go? What are you seeking?' And the unexpected reply was, 'Forgiveness, the ray of complete union with our Mother Spirit.' This was beyond me until I realized that I

141

was entering a calm such as I had never known. It was a calm in action. It was a sense of having reached or perhaps touched for a moment the very axle of life, or some pivot through which was passing a new vital flow of absolute stillness. It was uncanny, and I feared to lose this super harmony by some slip of my thought. So I prayed to the Spirit of Everest, the radiant figure I had seen twice before, and the reply came, 'You must evoke this sense out of your inner being. Your greater self will be your guide.'

Hitherto, I had been shown and felt all things coming from outside myself; now I was entirely at the mercy of my inner senses, such as I may have acquired. Dazed and stupid, I waited, while the earth vibrations were tapping on the walls of my thought, like a chicken in the egg helping me to break out of my insularity and force myself to become united with the greater me on another level of existence, for what seemed like an endless span of quiescent waiting, of constantly losing and recovering the line of thought. Then, quite suddenly, the pricking sensation ceased, and I was alone with an enlarged sense of the space around me, with a feeling that I and the space were one. I was outside my hitherto etheric body. I had no further need of it; I was above and within, I had ceased to be held by the earth vibration. I was free of earth and had become a space man!

This has not been expressed at all well, but it may give an inkling of the vastness and the fragrance of these stages of becoming.

*In the Autumn of 1973, Joe started his journeys to India and the Far East.*

I first met Gandhi up in the mountains, I was taken to his Ashram. He was sitting in prayer and sending thoughts into the minds of his closest followers, in very much the same way that I am doing this with you. I joined him and sat down to listen to his teaching. It was all very simple and quite sound. Then, when their physical bodies moved away he turned to me such a charming smiling face. He saw all that I was and had been in one second.

He bowed and said in a sad voice, 'We have all made many mistakes, and we always think that our own are the greater, but in the eyes of the All-Seeing One we are all still ignorant erring children. Now let us put the past away and work together.'

I nodded.

'You are a practical Englishman, and you see the physical needs of our people. I am a mystic who can see a little into the minds of men, and of the Greater Spirits, and can with your help pass wisdom into these suffering masses. Now let us be practical. When the belly is filled the mind is free to expand, but when the belly is empty there is but one thought: *food* – until the body shakes off the sense of hunger. This is a very wonderful moment, but often so transitory: unless we can get a tight hold on the mind, the body generally falls away; death occurs, and we are left to rescue and re-educate the spirit.

'But we have lost the opportunity to insert teaching into the bodily brain. So, I am going to ask you to stand with me when I insert my teaching, and you will by your strong physical link hold the physical and the spirit bodies together.'

I nodded in complete ignorance, and away we went into the hunger areas, and found ourselves again in an Ashram where an old priest was slowly dying of hunger. Gandhi began speaking to his spirit body, calming him, showing him visions of goodness knows what, until he became so charmed and happy, and would have floated out on to the next plane if I had not held tightly on to the cord which connects the bodies and kept him on the earth plane.

After a few moments Gandhi relaxed and so did I, and to my surprise, on looking down at our old priest, who had been just a shrivelled husk of humanity, I saw a sleeping man, quite well nourished and in perfect health!

I looked at Gandhi in amazement; he laughed and said, 'That is what we can do together, but we must unite.'

That was my first experience. Since then I have been through many more. Douglas often joins us and then he takes the part of Gandhi while I hold the physical, and the essence of life is poured back into the empty physical body, until it gains the power to live without food, just as Douglas did in that early life in France.

Well now I've spilt my beans and told you what I am doing. Lorny dear, I wonder if you'd give me a few thoughts on this line. All your thoughts are very useful, and you loved the Indians too. I call them all Indians. Pakistani is only a name, and all are suffering.

I see now that we have an immense power over all the people we have governed. Curzon is as active as ever and so is Kitchener. They've made up their quarrel and work together! But of the two Curzon is *my* man. I am devoted to him. He is still so human and full of wit and fun.

These really great men have established a link with India on this enduring plane for what seems like all time! Halifax told me that he knew this instinctively during life. He could feel that Curzon, with all his queer ways, was the forerunner of a great union between the East and the West.

I'd like to go on with this tomorrow if you aren't bored? I find it utterly absorbing.

\*   \*   \*

Cynth, I'm sorry I wasn't clear about the way in which I was working with Gandhi, or of the case of Douglas in France.

Now listen! We have or have had on the earth plane three bodies. The physical, which eats and sleeps and gets tired and is very tied up with earth in every sense. Yet it has links with the two other bodies, the astral, which is part physical, part etheric. This body usually escapes and disappears a few days after death, for it is the linking body. You might call it the home of the subconscious.

In the ordinary case of death you find the person in the astral body is able to see and hear all that is going on around him on earth, but without any clear perception of the next plane. Directly the perception of the next plane touches him the light of the spirit seems to burn up the astral, and the person gains knowledge and sight of the etheric plane, and ceases to have any strong link with the physical. Now this is where death and all the separateness comes in.

The great desire from those on the next plane is *now* to show you in the body, so that the transition need not be so drastic or complete. Here I am, talking easily with you, and using a tiny part of my astral body which has become etherialized, but it has kept a channel through which the physical energy can still flow. They feel this is vital now for the growth of the spirit in man. Man is searching wildly for new teaching. Here is the answer.

So, when I was working with Gandhi or Douglas, I was holding the astral cord, so that on waking, the old priest (in my first experience) found himself in a normal condition. He got up and continued his duties as a priest among the starving, dying people. *But*, he no longer needed food or rest, and he carried a certain radiance in his body, which was not perceptible in daylight; and he possessed powers to calm and heal the tortured souls. I do not know how long he or any of them are able to hold this condition.

\*     \*     \*

Let's go on talking about faith. I can't think why it was absent to such an extraordinary degree on earth among mankind, when I

145

now see – and I could have seen then – that all creation was living by faith. The trees shed their leaves, the flowers seem to die; all vegetable life seems to give up life every Autumn with such complete faith in the power of rebirth in Spring that before withdrawing they make their plans, and form their buds for the next year. But we can't believe that the same power will sustain us from day to day. And when, in a few rare instances, people have risked all upon faith in almighty power, it has been shown to work with amazing success.

Now this awful thing in Pakistan and India, the epidemic I've been sent over to see and listen to. They have faith in rebirth but no compassion for suffering. That is quite horrifying, even for me, or perhaps more so here, because we can see and smell the cruel unfeeling rays much more easily than you can. So I now understand how those rare people who give themselves completely to the cause of eradicating suffering in any form, animal or human, gather to themselves a spirit body of compassion which has very much the same vibration as the Christ Ray.

I see now how inextricably interwoven our mental and physical bodies are. Douglas took me into the children's tent in one of these refugee hospitals. The rain was making it all sodden, and it was leaking everywhere, causing the children to shiver from the sudden chill. Then, in came what we used to call a warm personality, who dispensed fun, laughter and food to these tired, frightened children, and they began to warm themselves by the sound of her voice which radiated warmth. She was a Pakistani, so she could speak their language and had a built-in love of children. This must be a Heaven-sent gift (I never had it!), but I see the way love in one personality can bring peace out of a chaos which seemed to me absolutely ghastly.

Douglas told me we must feed this woman with energy. I said *how*?

'Just stand near and radiate. You have learnt how to do this, so now you must do it. Throw your light over her, just as I threw it over my painting in France long ago.'

Well, you can imagine how clumsy I was. Douglas said I was radiating, but I hadn't learnt how to focus the light. I suppose a tiny flow of some sort was coming out of my body, but it was such a thin line of light that even when I stood quite close to her there seemed to be no way of making my light branch off into her aura. I turned helplessly to Douglas, but he had gone! And left me with this assignment!

I did my breathing as I'd been taught, and tried desperately to force my light into the woman's aura, but it only waved about or came out in lumps from my head and feet. Then I had the idea of getting it to pass out of my hands. More deep breathing, more concentration upon this unruly fluid light, and then suddenly I seemed to overcome a blockage, and it passed straight out of me – bang! And I hadn't any more left. I saw the light in her aura with great relief, but it left me with a sense of empty impotence.

I called to Douglas and he came back laughing at my dilemma, and showed me how to pass my empty hands over my head and shoulders, spine and diaphragm and reawaken the centres once more. I hadn't learnt about the chakras as he called them. But as I touched my head, throat, chest and diaphragm, I could see the light glowing again.

I said, 'This is all very well, but I just can't keep up the flow, it's all too slow.'

How he laughed! 'Running again before you can walk, Daddy,' was all the comfort I got. But on looking at my Pakistani patient, I saw she was still absorbing my nobbles of light, and was working on contentedly. The children had all stopped crying, some were laughing, others eating, and still others curled up asleep like a litter of puppies in complete contentment.

Well, this is just to show you what a lot of work and development lies ahead of me; and I have only mastered a tiny iota, before I am tossed into a new situation and told 'to act'! However those silly church hymns got written about eternal rest I just don't know. You won't have a moment's inaction here unless you particularly desire it. Which you know I never did!

So this is all for today, and good luck to my lessons! Lot of love, Lorny dear; how you will laugh to think of me working among a mass of filthy Indian children. Not quite my line on earth!

*　　*　　*

I want to go on with my very halting description, because this is one side of the great awakening, and I am so happy to be in on it, and upon my own ground, the Far East, which I was being prepared for during all those long years in China and Japan.

I told you about our journey through the mountains of Asia when we gathered the vibs from the mountain peaks and brought them to bear in a concentrated way upon the peasantry in the appropriate valley, blending them with the physical vibs of the people. They are all very simple and easily influenced. They live here with, by, and in close touch with the great earth spirits, and so to them the vision of a great Teacher was not unknown. It had often happened in their history, and even in their own personal experience. So, with the power, we began under careful direction to construct moulds into which higher spirits might become visible and audible. I was enormously interested to see how this could be done. So far I have myself seen some of the great initiates, but only for brief moments, my work has been with men whom I've known and admired – Van, Hugh, Alex and so on – most of all Gandhi; and now through him we were learning to concentrate the rays into a mass of light and colour; when this had been done to an intense degree I suddenly saw and felt that the light was pregnant with *life*.

A being of transcendant beauty was absorbing and gathering in all the tendrils of light into one body of celestial form. I was so intensely excited that I could have cried for joy.

'Don't be afraid,' said a voice that seemed to speak to me direct. 'I am now bringing you the Christ vibration to awaken and transmute the discords in the mountains. The Christ is everywhere at all times, but he needs the light and colour with which to mould his body into a living form to inspire and infuse the joy of living into all around. You may not be able to hold the vision for long; that is not necessary, but if you can carry the thread into the villages, some people will also see and hear me for a space of time, and once seen the vibration takes root in the aura and becomes a living part of *me*.

At this point the vision faded and I hurried into the nearest village holding the thought of this glorious being steadfastly in my mind. As I came into the little market place where people were buying and selling, I stood and waited, gathering the rays in my mind and holding them in a concentrated form until suddenly a child ran up to me and said, 'You are on fire, you are burning.'

People stopped what they were doing and stared at me, and the old priest of the village came close to me and making obeisance thanked me for bringing the Lord Buddha into shape and form. Others saw the being too and many were on their knees feeling a strange exhilaration, a lightening of the load of pain or anxiety. I held it for as long as I could, and then feeling that I was losing my power I dropped into a type of unconsciousness, and in that moment I was able to step consciously into another body of reflected light, and watch the effect the rest of our team were having.

*Joe's last post in the Diplomatic Service was in Moscow and he was tremendously interested in the Russian people.*

## COSMONAUTS – I

I've just been with the Cosmonauts who've come over to us from the Russian spacecraft. They are another instance of dogmatic thought wrecking the project. I don't know what actually went wrong with their bodies, but their minds were so unyielding that they could not and would not accept unexpected conditions. If these three had been in the American spacecraft that was brought down safely after a mechanical failure, they would probably not have died. But the American mind is far more flexible. It is mind over matter far more effectively true in outer space where weightlessness affects everything.

Having some Russian vibrations in my make-up I was able to get near them, and let a little light into their minds. They are such a nice trio and we are doing all we can, but these indoctrinated, all-powerful and self-sufficient minds are very hard to alter. It was the most amazing demonstration to me of indoctrination which must cede place to the Christ ray and not to annihilation, which the Russians expected and had built into their own minds.

Luckily one of them had an old relative who'd still held on to some vestiges of church teaching, some feeling for another and a greater power than the comintern, and this she pushed with all her might into the consciousness of her grandson. As he left his body she stood holding him up and saying *live – live –* you must *live*. The others were registering the death they had expected, but this boy came to very slowly with her arms round him. He was glad to see her, and forgot that she had passed over before him. His mind was still on the success of their flight.

'We did well, little Mother, didn't we?' he kept saying, and she praised him for all he'd done while trying to awaken life in him. But when he caught sight of the bodies of the other two he was frightened.

150

The capsule was opened and the bodies removed, his own among them. He clung to his 'Little Mother' and she to him, becoming as near physical as she could, calming him and making him see that he was alive and well.

She is still with him, now that he has relaxed into sleep; and I think later she will help his companions. But the lesson these accidents teach is that *mind* is the adjustable mechanism that can focus power of another sort. Prayer in space is so easy that the first message from the Americans when they landed on the moon was to read from the Bible. 'In the beginning was God. . . .' They knew and felt the immense power that was being put within the scope of ordinary God-believing man.

All very new to me – and quite a pipeful to think over!

I have been trying to keep the Cosmonauts asleep! You will wonder at this because you would expect them to sleep for at least some weeks. But the Russian set-up is quite different. They are beset by scientific knowledge. Science is the God of Russia. Well, that is one aspect of divinity, so their devotion works quite well, but it lacks the personal and humanist element, and this makes them into something very like robots of the mind.

So, once they'd left their bodies and found they were alive outside the capsule, and able to pass through into and out of the capsule without any friction, they were astounded and ready with pencils and paper to work out the pressure of air gravitation, etc. They got the idea that owing to having been in space for so long they had, as it were, passed through another sound barrier; only in this case it was a barrier which brought freedom from gravitation down to earth. All this time they completely ignored their own physical bodies and I wondered if they actually saw them – they were so much absorbed by this new power to pass through solid matter and still remain above the earth surface.

When the doors were opened and the ground crew removed the bodies they naturally tried to speak to them with no successs. Then ensued a commotion. Russian voices were raised, and raised, and *raised*, and owing to their insistence they became quite insensible to us and could see only the physical plane and were exultant over their newly-acquired power but furious that no one noticed them.

We stood by until the *cortége* taking the bodies had gone; and then it began to dawn on them that somehow they'd got out of their bodies as other spacemen had walked in space on other occasions. So they got back into the capsule to talk things over and, reaching no conclusion, they dropped off to sleep before passing into the usual stage of being able to 'see' on our plane.

But the sleep was only a superficial unconsciousness and they were soon awake again, and this time they woke to find us with them and very unwillingly they began to register a change in everything. At one moment they were lying in their places in the capsule, then suddenly there was no capsule and they were on the grass, and the sun and wind was stirring their hair and faces. Still they went on with figures and drew us into the discussion.

Then one of them suggested that they should go home and see what effect they made on their families. 'But we've no transport,' one of them said. However, since there were various jeeps within view I suggested we took over one of them, and then we were able to transport them instantly, delivering each one at his own home. I stayed with one of them. He was delighted to be back. He rushed in and kissed his wife who at first showed no reaction. She had just received news of his death and she was utterly stunned with misery – and then for a moment – a wonderful moment – they both saw and felt the presence of each other. Her face lighted up as she said, 'How could they tell me that you are dead?' and then flung herself into his arms. A few seconds later she knew, alas, that she was holding empty air – but the reality was so real that we were able to feed her with the conviction that her man was alive.

After this tremendous effort he relaxed into the sleep that should have come earlier and we took him on to the etheric plane of awakening, where I shall be in attendance when he wakes.

I was very glad to be able to take part in this – something after my own heart in many respects and putting me in close touch with Russia and all it has meant to me in the pasts, yes, several of them. I felt a great friendliness for the Russian people and had I known the language there would have been no strangeness between us.

# WEIGHTLESSNESS

This is good. You've been thinking on another plane of thought lately. I am so glad. It's always difficult to insert a new vibration, and you have just taken on the view that anti-gravitation might become a thing in your physical life. Many people who you know have this power already: of course, Andrew had it well established before he left the body. Now you must train your mind to accept the power of movement in and out of the body. This change must come gradually, otherwise the whole planet would fly to bits, and chaos on a very fast scale would be the result. Weightlessness – that is the theme. Try and see yourself as weightless.

I know it's hard to take up a new idea of this kind but it's much easier to route new ideas in the physical before you come over entirely into the etheric. It makes progress so much quicker. You've no idea how awkward I felt when it was imposed upon me. I slipped out of my body into one exactly similar and used it in the same way, feeling *grand*. Then came the moment of decision. I saw I was not of the same texture as Pat and Douglas and asked why, and they explained ruthlessly that I hadn't died yet and was still completely physical! So I must face the second death of virtually pushing off this nice comfortable physical body that was diseaseless and fatigueless and take on the Christ vibration of timeless, spaceless energy. I wasn't at all impressed. I wanted to stay as I was. And so I did for a long time, learning to use my physical body which was not suited to space travel until I became restless and longed to go further.

Had I accepted the weightlessness when in the body I could have acquired this on leaving the old one immediately, instead of going through all this intermediate stuff. Of course, many people – oh! – millions, just stay in their ex-physical body until it literally wears out or is reabsorbed into spirit; then there is no alternative but either to reincarnate or go on into the finer vibrations.

I chose the latter, but after soul-searching quests. I did not want to be separated from you and, of course, Lorna, and if I went into a reincarnating body, that would separate us for a further period. No – you and Lorna were not so far away through the help of your pen, and if and when you come over, which can't be very long

154

delayed, then we should all be belonging and growing together.

It's the great strength of the group soul within us that forced me in to this. You can't think how agonizing it was to push off my old, much loved physical remnant of a body and say goodbye for always and ever and become vaporized. That is what it means. I said, 'I will do this', and Douglas and Pat, both now high Initiates, were able, with Flo's help, to drag me – the real *me* – out of all the soft friendly acts and encounters of the physical. It was an experience, I can tell you. Now I'm very glad I've been through it, but at the time it felt like annihilation. This is what I ask you both to avoid by accepting the flow of weightlessness into your mind body.

Now – see yourself rising off your bed as you go to sleep. You do this unconsciously. Do it consciously. In meditation push your finer body out of your physical. See and feel yourself passing from room to room, from person to person, as you do on the healing ray. See yourself in the hospital or the private house with your patients.

We are just welcoming the Arch Healer, Harry Edwards, over here. He is a great fellow. What a lot of barriers he has contested and overcome. Life on earth holds so much that it is difficult to decide to give it up. But no one hurries you, so for aeons of time, one can go on living in a half and half body, seeing and doing all the old physical things plus the enormous expansion of consciousness. But I wanted to go on and so will you. Accept this idea and work upon it, and the seed will be sown in your finer body ready to be used on waking over here.

*At this time I could sense a certain boredom in my brother with all this endless healing, and a great longing to escape and seize the opportunity of climbing Everest.*

Just think of starting off to scale Everest with neither training nor equipment. But why not? My new body does not respond to cold, fatigue or height. So we started. We could have gone straight to the summit, but that was not my idea. I wanted to follow the route of the climbers. Gandhi saw my desire and fell in with it. So we started from the foot hills, where masses of lovely flowers and shrubs were growing.

Gandhi paused at the head of one of the great valleys and said, 'Now, before climbing we will absorb the strength and beauty of the flowers.'

I watched his aura as he drew colour and scent from them, and then got up and walked on. Yes, we walked, or rather we seemed to slip over the ground. The heights were fun and when we reached the cliffs where many of the climbers faltered, we just drifted up the side in marvellous weightless ease.

Each mountain top possessed its own earth spirit. Gandhi saluted them each in turn, asking for their help, not only for our climb, but for his work among the animals and peoples of India.

After what seemed a short time we reached the lower slopes of Everest. This is quite something even in the etheric. It's a terrifying mountain! How I admire Hunt and all his men who faced up to such a challenge in the physical body. I just don't know how they came to succeed. The long slogging road to the foot, and then this colossal mountain with all its hazards.

To me, of course, there were no hazards, but the great Spirit of the Mountain does not welcome humanity except in a very advanced form. This I learned from Gandhi who explained that he could not let me climb alone. I should have lost my way and returned without seeing any of the peaks; they would have withdrawn and shrouded themselves in mist; but his coming dispelled all the unfriendly aspects, so that I was made to feel at one with all nature. Nature can do this everywhere, but here in the Himalayas the withdrawal can be vicious.

These heights have been kept sacred to admit only certain vibs. The Sherpa who made the summit with Hunt knew this; he belonged to the country and together with their superb courage they were granted success.

*       *       *

How can I tell you about the last and most wonderful experience of all time for me – our rising to the summit!

During this last phase I was sensing the emotion and the physical efforts of those two climbers, and around me in the ether I was being shown the defences of the mountain. Dante's Inferno of fiend voices shrieked and brushed past us. I looked at Gandhi, he remained motionless, but I could see he was strangely stirred by the horror and the force which surrounded this master peak.

Eventually we slid through a bank of blackness, emerging suddenly into a world of light.

Here at last was the roof of the world. The beauty and the strength of all the surrounding peaks seemed to flow into this great power centre of Everest.

I cannot describe the charm or the grandeur, or the immense thrill of standing on the crest of this great mountain, or explain the soul-surrendering flashes that swept through me as I tried to absorb the wonder of this experience. I knew that I was reaching the point of unconsciousness due to over reception of far more advanced vibs than I could take into my system.

I turned to Gandhi and saw at once that he was seeing a beyond far in advance of my comprehension. I waited, holding on to consciousness with difficulty in this flaming vortex of light and sound. At first the sound was too obscure and abstract for me to fathom. It resembled mountain torrents, but as I waited it changed into fragments of almost earthly music reminiscent of the old masters, then changing again with elfin glee into something that spoke of snow and ice and the blue heaven.

Then, suddenly, it all changed and I received what I can only describe as a bearable rapture which descended upon me, and I saw a figure of light so transcendant that I was blinded and could only sense the semi-transparent wonder of this marvellous Presence.

Was it the spirit of the mountain or Christ Himself? I do not know; I shall probably never know.

This is the greatest experience I have ever had.

I've been exploring the whole of the Himalayan range, right up into China and Tibet and on into Persia. You've no idea of the wealth of power expended by these peaks, but, as you know, they select the recipients very carefully!

Lately I've been learning, under Gandhi's supervision, how to pass down into India some of the less concentrated rays from Everest. It's rather a slow business; we have first to empty our auras, (not a very easy thing) and become absolutely neutral to all but the white lights. This is very important. If one empties one's aura without careful training, one lets in the lower vibrations straight away. It took me a long time to devise a method of my own to tune in only to the white rays. Pat and Douglas were much more advanced, and could do this at once, so they helped me, since I couldn't possibly have done it alone. My physical vibrations are still very potent and useful for passing on this suffusion of light into the Ashrams and other places tuned to receive it.

So far as I can see the Himalayas are the greatest force for good in the whole geographical world, and their psycho-spiritual output is colossal. I went on to Japan and tested Fuji.

All these mountains have at one time or another, or, as in the case of Fuji, constantly, been looked upon as divine; and they are in almost every case the mouthpiece of divine inspiration. Fuji has the accumulated prayers of many centuries, and you can draw this multi-racial, multi-religion power from her quite easily, especially as you know Fuji. Remember everything you can about the mountain, see it in all its different phases, and then with a mounting sense of personal union *see* the top of the peak on fire with light. Draw that fire into your own aura to glow and reflect upon all who come near you. Later, when you have established this fire, you can send it on into the auras of people whom you want to help.

This goes for a very large number of the mountains that I've visited. But not all. There are also those invested by a negative power, and under the influence of these mountains much cruelty has arisen. There are some in central Asia from which stem enormous roots of negative force. Where there is white magic you will nearly always find the equivalent in some form directed against the God Power.

My first experience was in China. I had no idea when I perched myself on the summit of a peak ready to open my centres to draw in; then I suddenly noticed that the mountain was emitting horrible black smoke. I thought at once of an eruption; then I remembered that I was looking into the etheric, and Pat sent me a long-distance warning that I must close the centres of my aura, and brace myself against the darker powers. In another moment she and Douglas were beside me, and I felt rather like a naughty boy who'd gone into the larder without leave! She instantly threw a strong blue ray all over the three of us as we stood on the pinnacle – and we waited.

I said, 'Well, what do we do now?'

'Wait, and emit all the white power you can. We must not only save you but also the mountain. Here, for centuries, have been imprisoned the entities of those who have done much evil; but they have mostly expiated their sins and are ripe for release. That is why you came here, led unconsciously by their need.'

I felt slightly less guilty, but very uncertain of my power to hold the white light. The dark smoke was suffocating us, and I saw no light. Then at the worst moment when I was almost fainting, Douglas and Pat emitted a ray of dazzling white light, which was instantly reflected by numerous other peaks and points of light all over the vast expanse of mountains before and beneath us. I simply gasped. The whole of my body was quaking with the unexpected contest of light and darkness, which was taking place within and around me. The frightful noise was deafening, but with the light came *calm*, and as we three stood together I sensed that the battle had been won and the mountain cleansed of these horrible vibrations for ever. . . .

Very slowly they gathered me up with them and we moved off to Fuji for rest and recovery. It has been a soul-rending experience, and one which they say must be repeated over and over again before the earth is cleansed and able to absorb the white light completely.

I went to Fuji, having been several times before when in this body, and I went alone. I felt the vastness of it and the almost terrifying power. I did not want to go alone again, so, with Hugh, Douglas and Arthur we started working upon the Japanese peasants in the surrounding villages. It was all quite different from the Chinese and Tibetan vibs. Here there had been distinct interference by the negative forces. I think it was from Fuji's negative side that most of the brutal war measures of the last war were framed. The greater the power for good, the greater also for the less good.

The Great Earth Spirit was fighting for supremacy, and the negative channel of Fuji was eventually subdued. But that was not enough.

When I first visited Fuji, it felt like a great leviathan of power in a quiescent state. I feared to stir a leaf or stone; the silence was deep and pregnant with subdued wrath. Yes, that was the Fuji I first met, and I left it very willingly.

As we continued our work among the villagers we began to make way slowly with them. There were among them those who had fought in the last war and been in contact with the negative ray and used as carriers of that ray of destruction. But there were others who were still impregnated with the inner rays of Fuji, to whom war was a revulsion; and to them we turned in their sleep bodies in order to cure the sickness in those others who were still suffering from the negative ray.

At first it was a hard proposition, but when those holding the inner rays of white light fused them with our own, the barrage of light became too strong for the others to withstand; and so they left the villages and went to other places to work, which they found more attractive. Families split up and there was a general feeling of upheaval, but in the end we had enough power actually to enter the mountain. This was a most fantastic adventure.

By this time we had attracted some really great spirits of the angelic nature. I do not know their names, but they are beautiful beyond description. I think they are called the Avatars. When I saw that they were taking over the enterprise, I felt myself renewed with power. It is wonderful to be actually working with

161

these enormously advanced beings of light. Some of the villagers actually saw them, and were so excited they said that Buddha had returned to lead them into Nirvana . . . and that the end of the world had come!

But, of course, seed time and harvest still had to go on laboriously, keeping them within the daily rhythm of toil and everyday life. But the light grew around them and around us as we entered the mountain under the leadership of these great beings.

I had the strong sensation that Fuji was dead, inert and empty. We had the whole strength of the village with us. They were of course in their sleep bodies, but none the less impregnated with the vibrations of the mountain, and they formed the link for the Great Ones, and forced the entry on the material plane. So, you see, the simplest tools can be used for the most colossal undertakings.

Once inside the etheric stronghold the Avatars flashed the whole light of Christ, Buddha, Zoroaster, Vishnu and all the Deities of the surrounding peaks, forming a blaze of sound and light that was more than I could tolerate. I was bemused and almost unconscious, saying to myself – so this is the war in Heaven. The chaos of light and sound was so terrific that I think I must have lost consciousness for a time. I knew I could do nothing, it had all been carried on to a plane beyond my knowledge or apprehension. Hugh and Arthur felt the same, and we could only await the final issue.

Suddenly the light grew soft and a great silence fell upon us, a silence such as I had never known – redolent with majestic power. We knelt down and gave ourselves into its keeping.

That is all I can put into words. We were gradually withdrawn from the vicinity of the mountain, and our spirit bodies which had been drawn out of our normal etheric shells returned to their habitual proportions, and I, Joe, became just myself again, no more and no less.

So the Angelic Host left us. But they had not left us completely empty handed, and I knew that this experience was a sort of initiation, and we shall be a little nearer to those Great Ones when the next crisis comes our way.

# SENSING THE LIFE OF THE JAPANESE PEASANTS

In meditation here we open ourselves, breathing in the force and becoming like an immense funnel. That is exactly what we all look like in meditation or prayer, and so do you. You form consciously or unconsciously an etheric V-shaped funnel over your head through which the power flows into you, and out through your brain, hands, eyes and breath. I've been taught a thing or two over here! I wish I'd known more of this when I was working with the F.O. So often I stumbled against a wall of 'unknowing' when I might have drawn in confidence and unconscious 'knowing' to illuminate my path.

I was talking this over with Van, and he said he had acquired the 'unconscious knowing', and accepted it without question, adding, 'We couldn't see the deep causes when in the physical body, but we could "apprehend" them, and that is what you are being asked to do now; it is, in fact, the essence of faith made a little more concrete.'

I've been wandering about among my old colleagues in the places in which we served, especially China and Japan; but I have also been to Budapest, and throughout the communist countries. It was there that I first met your friend Andrew. How I like him, (nothing churchy about him!) but radiant with outgiving power. He is one of our band and comes very often to Everest and the other centres.

You remember I was asked to help reignite the mountains in China and Japan. This is a vast work and I have had to enlist an enormous new staff, mainly from their own locality. I had to learn more about the language patterns of all the different Chinese dialects. This isn't as difficult as it sounds, because we have thought transference to back up our visual intake.

I was enormously interested in really seeing the life of the Chinese peasant in the mountain villages; their co-operation is vital, because they are exuding the vibs from the surrounding mountains, and form our very best physical link. But apart from that I *love* the Chinese peasant, he is so rough, and yet so understanding. He seems to have been born with a built-in sense for mountain worship. But besides all that, it is so delightful to

163

move about without the sense of cold, dirt and fatigue, which always accompanied physical travel!

I spend many nights in the villages conversing with their etheric bodies, while the physical ones are asleep; and when they wake up and the bodies become united again I carry the sum total of their allegiance to the great mountain spirits around their particular valley.

Tomorrow I will tell you about Fuji and how the mountains respond.

Cynth, good girl, I do want to write to Lorna. Things are growing very tense in your world, and we have to come closer and closer to your plane in order to avoid open war. We have to hold the opposing factions in opposition to each other, and balance the forces to promote peace. It's not the peace of God, it is only the balance of power. Everything in all your planes of physical life depends upon balance, magnetic, emotional and biological in one sense or another, and the magnified powers here have to be balanced accordingly.

I have had to learn all this in order to deal with the power centres. It becomes more and more profoundly interesting.

Take, for instance, Fuji which we both know. This is not one immense power centre but clusters and clusters of large and small whirlpools of energy. How to disentangle them and cleanse them, when the whole field of action was revealed to me seemed at first to be an absolutely hopeless task. But I was told: 'nothing is hopeless with the Spirit of God. Work at the beginning, start from the bottom of the ladder and don't look too far ahead.'

So I took some of the lower slopes. Van came with me and several others, all from the Service. We entered the tiny whirlpools of power and sensed their condition. Some were completely under the subservience of a negative earth force opposing the positive earth force in which the human vibration did not enter. This was our job. The soil on these slopes should have been fertile and productive, but owing to this imbalance it was entirely negative, and had no power to give life. So, we, who are outside the body, had to induce the physical landworker or peasant to hazard an attempt to plant and cultivate hitherto unproductive soil, and by their positive thinking draw out the negative and impose the positive through their bodily vibrations into the soil. You've no idea how fertilizing the human mind can be in recasting the vibrations through the physical channel direct into the soil.

We tried at first with some old hardened veterans of farm work, but their minds were closed to the possibility of good crop from poor soil. 'It never had yielded so why should it begin now?' Then we found a young couple, keen and eager and full of vitality. We set the circumstances for them to farm these barren wastes, and almost immediately the germ of life began to take form, and the virginity of the soil gave out at the same time a tiny vibration of psychic energy which flowed into the great spiritual channel which exists in the ether almost everywhere.

Well, that's a lesson in transmutation. For some time I have been working all out on this project. It's very absorbing and has many diverse uses. Animal welfare comes under one heading; the healing of all human infirmities physical and mental comes into another category, so one is never bored by repetition. I have to make constant journeys to Everest and Chartres with certain vibs, and sometimes out into the upper ether. But this is another story.

# JOE'S MEETING WITH HIS GREATER SELF

I want to tell you about my old lives, the one in Iona in particular, when Columba, or 'I Columkill', was my leader and guide. I have mentioned him before but not by name. I didn't know who he was, except that he was a very far advanced person, in those days when I sailed his boat and listened to his stories and his glorious singing voice.

Now you are all nearing the stage when our past lives make sense. It's just like a jigsaw puzzle; sometimes it's all chaos and then suddenly one piece explains the whole thing. Well, I am allowed to tell you this. All of us who have grasped and understood the meaning behind this chaotic physical plane, are now going through the last round of this particular exercise, and unless you particularly wish to return there will be no more physical bodies for you to live in. Your world is changing and should you return in some aeons of time it will be to a completely different, and less material existence.

We all try to help those on the physical plane as I am helping you at present. But I too have finished my term. I'm half sorry, I've enjoyed a lot of it, but I loathed much more; so I close the book of earthly physical lives without regret, but with immense interest, because I can now piece some of it together.

The first war was the opening of my eyes to pain, misery and murder, and the uselessness of it all. Then my life as a diplomat sought to build up in my mind the need to reconstruct the world as an evolutionary machine. Of course I never thought of it along those lines, but my greater soul was forever sorting and sieving the results, and when I came over here I made contact with this other Joe! Rather an awkward *mauvais quart d'heure* was spent while we levelled up to each other. I was surprised and ignorant and rather aggressive to this other *me* who took for granted so much that you had tried to explain, while the lesser Joe continued to say, 'Well, that's all fine and large but give me proof.' And so he did. I wish you could have been there! I was shown the evolution of both Joes, how one came into material life while the other remained in pure spirit; one often pulling against the other.

The meeting with my Upper Joe took place on Iona. I had a

167

sense of expansion that seemed always to herald another phase of development; I had grown used to these changes and had been through several. Gandhi explained them and prepared me for each in turn until I came to Iona. I had been going through my old lives at Craignish and Scarba, and on to the comparative safety and freedom of life on Iona, when suddenly, as the sense of expansion grew, I was conscious of a being beside me fashioned in some ways on the same mould. I turned and looked at him and I said at once, 'Oh, you must have been my brother Oliver whom I never saw in earth life.'

'No,' he replied, 'I am yourself.'

'But,' I stammered, 'I'm still *me*. What do you mean?'

'Yes, and I'm still *you* and myself, one and the same. I have been your light reflection all through your earth life, and now we can be re-united.'

I wasn't at all sure that I was in favour of this getting together, and said so. He merely laughed and said, 'You don't quarrel with your hands and feet, and you'll be a much more complete Joe if we are united.'

'Well, how do we do it?' I asked.

'Don't be in a hurry. You must learn to accept me first as your shadow or reflection. But I only reflect the highest in you.'

This disturbed me greatly; 'There isn't very much of the higher as you call it in me.'

'Well I find there is,' was the unexpected reply; 'I am the result of your effort and industry and uprightness, together with your fundamental love for the people around you. Oh, I know lots of them irritated you beyond bearing, but you did bear with them, and all that has built up an entity which is *me*. Now you see I am entirely *you*, so you can't throw me out or brush me off. I am *you* cleaned up, and ready to receive the higher vibrations: how do you take that? I'm a sort of bank balance on the credit side.'

'Well, I'm awfully glad to hear that I have a bank balance, and of course I accept you as part of myself; I suppose as you are the upper boy you'll take command.'

I didn't like the idea of jettisoning *my way*. But he only laughed and said, 'Trust me. I won't usurp your will; we can co-operate quite easily.'

And so the oddest sort of marriage began between the two *me's*, and I found I was enormously but *enormously* changed, stronger, happier, richer by far in understanding and in correlating events and the purposes behind them. And so I was able to take on these missions to and from Everest and Chartres, which the lesser Joe could never have undertaken.

# EXPEDITION TO EVEREST IN SEARCH OF
# THE FORGIVENESS RAY

Cynth, how extraordinarily refreshing to be writing with you
again. Life surges on around one here in great waves of movement, and one needs, I repeat *needs* the power of returning and
just talking to people in the physical body. You don't know how
important you are to us. Douglas and I have been discussing this
point. It's been entirely overlooked by the Christian churches in
spite of the fact that Christ came back several times in Biblical
history and many many more times that are not recorded, to show
how important we all are to each other. No one here should be
without the physical link, and inversely you in the body should
never lack the power to link with someone in the etheric. The
awful results of this isolation are shown to you continually by
people who ask for messages to be sent through you and not
through themselves. Faith is the rarest thing!

I've been with your Father Andrew. All your friends from this
side seek me out, and we have become quite a large group. He is a
very important link, and such good company. How he makes me
laugh! Born into the aristocracy in Poland, brought up like us on a
vast estate, and then giving it all up for an ideal! Crazy I should
have called it – but not now! He has a school over here; at first it
was for his own people, tenants and friends from the old estate
who loved and revered him for going into the Church, and for his
tremendously clever Scarlet Pimpernel activities!

Oh yes, he used all his powers physical, psychic and spiritual to
save everyone he came into contact with, and who were willing to
be saved, either upon your side or upon ours. If they died in prison
or from assassination he wriggled out of his body, and was with
them at the moment of death and awakening. He has gathered a
group on our side to meet and reconstruct life for those who went
over, and there were many; and they in turn have joined the group
who are now working with him in Poland.

I went with him on one of these expeditions to help and secure
and cleanse the sufferers. I saw the all-pervading obstacle to their
freedom was forgiveness. They can't forgive any more than the
Irish. So, in order to help, a new ray has to be anchored to the earth

plane. This is the last in the spectrum. It is the amethyst or purple ray, and once this can become absorbed into the aura forgiveness becomes possible.

How to generate enough of this ray is the real problem. Even Andrew could only produce a very tiny output. So we put the question over to Flo who said at once: 'Go back to Everest and find it.' So back we went with Hugh and Pat and Douglas and many others.

Some of us had already become regular visitors to those sunscape peaks, and we are accepted, if not actually welcomed; but to demand the use of such a vital ray from the heart of such a treasury was almost more than a 'Queen's Messenger' could expect! We had been merely tapping the outer covering of the riches held there. Nevertheless we entered the Realm of Light and laid our problem before the Etheric Throne. The great spirit keepers joined us, including Gandhi, and we were allowed to enter the mountain. This is more than I can explain today; let us write again tomorrow.

*       *       *

How to produce the ray which makes forgiveness possible? It's the heart of the Christ ray, and no one can live without some form of it and be happy. It's the ray that takes away all the grit in our unpleasant thinking, and for this new project we were urged to battle our way into the fastness of the Everest stronghold!

Flo came with us and, of course, Father Andrew. He was so excited and fascinated by the approach to this great mountain that I was afraid he would still be talking to the nature spirits on the surface when our chance came (if it did come), to enter the mountain. You see, I am still a doubting Thomas, and I still have these lapses! But Flo was quite calm and very, very confident.

As we stood on the shining plateau between the shining peaks, I

171

saw the etheric rocks yield into a mist of light revealing again the great figure of light seen on my first visit. This time I was able to raise my eyes to the glistening wonder of his being, and actually hear some of the message which Hugh, Andrew and Flo all received in full.

We were to follow and receive what could now be given. That was the gist of the message. The ground beneath us seemed to quiver, and yet remain firm. There was no sense of falling; it was more a feeling of changed surroundings. And then the light suffusion in which we stood seemed to take on the colour we were seeking, something akin to amethyst, but of a shade that I had never seen before. It radiated into our auras, and into our etheric bodies, and appeared to remake all our contacts with each other and every living tie we'd ever known. All sense of injury of any kind left us; it brought also the power to accept forgiveness. This was very potent especially for me. We have been dragging with us all these years the sense of injury inflicted by us, which is far worse than any injury incurred. But now this living oil had soaked up all the misery within us, and I knew that I could accept Lorna's wonderful forgiveness and become a whole man again.

How long we remained soaking our innermost selves in this most wonderful of all experiences I have no idea. But at a certain point the colour was withdrawn, the light became golden, and then white, and we were again among the topmost peaks of this gorgeously satisfying beauty which was now in some strange way more intimately ours. I suppose our receptive reach had been extended.

Andrew looked, and I believe is already one of the Christed Ones. I could see in him an approach to the shining figure who'd led us to the ray, and from that moment we accepted his leadership unquestioningly.

So, we returned to Chartres, our focal point, carrying what we were able of this most precious ray. Father Andrew went off to other centres, of which I believe Iona and Poland were among those he touched with the ray, while the rest of us were content to store this precious vibration within the precincts of Chartres, and try to realize all that had happened to us.

# Part VI

*Letter from Sir Ronald Fraser.*
*Letters from and about Lord Dowding*

What am I about? Well, when one comes over here one learns to divide one's radiations; we can use different bodies. We can go out simultaneously to different planes and peoples. We have to learn in the vastness of this new life that one must conserve one's radiations or they will be squandered until one has the power to produce an enormous quantity.

As to decision making. Decisions are the privilege of earth. I see now how I used to squander radiations on silly things and often allowed the vital issue to escape. But one can always do it again. I don't mean through another incarnation. Heaven forbid! I don't think many of us will do that again.

There are so many new forces about to be unleashed that we all long to warn you. Conserve your mental and physical energy. It will be needed.

I see you, Cynthia, have been probing into the possible disasters or victories of the future. Earth is ending – or nearing the end of a cosmic day which in this case synchronizes with the end of an Age and the entrance into the Aquarian Age. Such times are always times of great distress and unawareness. We place great interest in what you call the Saucer Folk. They are very definitely on your side. See them, invite them, and learn from them. They are far more advanced than you are and they may be able to defend the White Islands which as you know are the British Isles.

I've met your brother, Cynthia, and I know he is working on the lines between Chartres and Everest. As you know, Chartres is one of my greatest and nearest power points and my present work is to help in sifting and dispersing the power which issues both from Chartres and the Himalayas. All the time I was translating that book* I knew I was reliving one of my own lives as a builder and architect, and I gradually remembered how the plan came to me, waking and sleeping, without any understanding of mathematics or geometry. It came and was there. I had no need to question,

* Sir Ronald Fraser translated *Les Mystères de Chàrtres* by Louis Charpentier.

175

only to put the stones which I saw so clearly in my mind. Now when I see architects sweating over plans I long to say 'Relax!' and think as I did. Let the picture come through you. The ability has come back to me now and when any problem occurs I relax and ask for the great Powers to work through me. If only this technique was used more. The thing to do is to make all preparations first, that you can physically. I cut and collected the stone and left the unmasking of the design entirely to the greater Powers. People feel they must do it all themselves, while here on this level lie the greatest forces for achievement on any plane.

It is so nice to go on talking like this. I want to tell you how we are developing Chartres – no, not like planning committees, but on our plane, using and fusing the water, the air and the earth around the building into one mass of greater edifices which you will see one day. Chartres is now a city of cathedrals and each one is there for a separate purpose.

*[The next day]*

Good morning to both of you. This is splendid. Now come with me into the new Chartres. I am very proud of it, and a number of people in the body have seen and are using it subconsciously.

First we began by drawing from the very ancient temple far down below the present Church. We drew from the Aztecs. That may surprise you but the Aztecs were immensely strong in their vibrations. They were primitive and so they used the blood vibration which gave them access to many others. We took these and purified them through contact with the blood of Christ. This was absolutely the most exciting thing I have ever seen. The light meeting the darkness and completely routing it in a vortex of colour power.

So, we had the material for our new construction. What should be the aim and object of the new buildings? They were to follow the form already used, the pointed arch, the spire and the circle. The main object was to open a wide channel for the etheric to enter the physical church and then to produce further chapels towards the higher planes. As we grew the plan and drew the plan

176

on the ether in colour, form and sound, you've no idea what a jumble of beauty it created: not the hammer and chisel of former builders but the projection of thought-revealing forms which I had never seen and cannot describe. The first of these projections was a glorious building of domes and spires. It comprised the vibrations of East and West. We had many Buddhists and Sufis and other religious thinkers with us and when the etheric flow was moving we began using the channels in the form of aisles leading out in all directions. Some were drawing from the more primitive African faiths into union. Some were going out into the desert to the Mohammedans and along the Arabian coast. The world seemed to be entwined by these thought lines and connected with the central Power centre of Chartres.

You'll be interested to hear that our little black Madonna, so-called, from a distant age and faith is now a most potent figure. She is, or was (but time is not), the reincarnation behind the Madonna, or Mother of Christ, in a later period. A most wonderful, enthralling creature, blazing with the feminine vibration of all the ages and most arresting. I might say seductive, but that word does not live on this plane.

In taking you beyond the etheric plane I run out of language. We are then among the super faculties for which you have no words. But I can and will paint their form and beauty into your dreams.

Have I given you any idea of the majesty and grace of this most *formidable* edifice? I have never imagined its like on any plane and the love power is supersonic in all directions. It is like a vast river of God-Christ power.

I think I must leave it there, but I would like to add a footnote. Those who help us are from all ages and all planes including the Saucer People, as you call them. They give and receive like all of us from this vortex of ineffable power.

*Extract from a letter from Joe*

I've been seeing quite a lot of Hugh Dowding, and he drew me with him over to the USA about this Lockheed row. It was fascinating to see our side at work on a big industrial project. Of course Hugh was all for R.R. He knew the designers and admired their work, and said it was far and away the most advanced engine in the air, and the new methods adopted would open the way to a lot more research on quite a different line if it was accepted. Hugh is always full of enthusiasm.

Hugh says that through the knowledge of speed, we are gaining a new etheric sense in the body, and that the greater our conquest of space and speed, the more channels we are opening in the human aura towards the acceptance of things quite outside the track of ordinary human thinking. That is what youth is trying to do now in their rebellion against the rat race. In all the mess and instability of life, humanity is growing up. At least, that is his view.

I've been with you to Craignish (Argyll), it's a good place to meet and you heard me calling you. The seals were there and the curlews and all the gulls. Yes, it's a Devic place of high quality.

There is so much I would like to tell you. I find that most of my crowd seem to have learnt a good deal after coming over. We none of us guessed the intensity of loving or of being loved. One simply cannot face the earthly callousness and indifference to suffering mental and physical.

I've been with that friend of your brother's known as Van, a most advanced person. How immensely intricate is his knowledge of the channels of development. I knew him slightly before and now I find we are in the same group, and I am honoured and grateful to serve under him.

We have a most heterogeneous group, many diplomats, (including your brother), and people like Halifax, whom I also knew. He is away beyond me, but tremendously influential. We all grow and develop under the immediate influence of each other. Someone actually came and thanked me for the help he'd been given through my vibrations! No one was more astonished than I! I must pause now and write again later, thank you very much.

\*     \*     \*

Cynthia, I am glad to have this chance, you've not been writing very much lately, don't lose touch with us, it's a most important moment and there are very few of you about.

Yes, I am having a very interesting time, I have been among the planets and sized them up in my own way, and realized that we are a very small solar system, but it is ours, and we have been given a leading role in the development and growth of this system; no mean project, and extremely exciting.

These other planets are composed so differently, that is the amazing part; it remains for us to help construct thought bodies and perhaps psychic bodies which are able to live and to work and grow under quite different conditions. Some of the bigger planets are almost unformed, where we can grow the etheric or astral forms who evolve with the planet. Neptune and Uranus come into this category; while on earth we are creating the minds with which to fashion these advancing worlds.

It's a great project, when our earth seems to be in such turmoil, but the output of advanced souls from these conflicting areas is enormous. They seem to conclude their physical evolution here and then go on to the astral and the etheric to work on the next planet of their choice.

Very many have been chosen from India because of their advanced astral and etheric bodies. Here in Europe we are so practical and down to earth that to us is given the power to enter the auras of Mars and Venus.

I should like to write more about this later.

*When my brother was asked to return to Everest and bring back to Chartres the vibrations from the great peaks he was asked to choose someone to accompany him. He chose Lord Dowding, and the following is the latter's reaction from his first expedition.    C.S.*

Cynthia: I should like to go on with my first letter, and tell you how I experienced this extraordinary expedition to Everest with your brother.

I have always had a great affinity for mountains, but like your Joe, I never had the time or opportunity to climb or see any of the big mountains intimately. I had seen the Himalayas, and flown among the lower slopes, and looked upon them as almost as unattainable as Heaven upon earth. Now, I possess the open sesame to so much. Too much – far too much; so I take it in slowly with enormous overpowering enjoyment, which in this case, amounted to ecstasy. I suppose I was blundering about in the regions half physical, half ether, when I met your brother, and he told me of his new assignment. He has fallen in love with Everest. The magnetic pull of this great mountain has entirely captured him for the time being, and he has been used to help others to see and enjoy – and draw from this great power reservoir.

Owing to his passionate love for these peaks, and with Gandhi's help, he is now *persona grata* in those highlands which encompass human thought. I was most excited by all he told me, and caught the fire of his enthusiasm, and asked him at once if I could join one of these parties; and so I found myself skimming up the valleys and lower slopes, until we reached the enormous obstacles at the foot of the great climb. I was used to etheric travel by this time, and ready for the easy lifting power of thought to carry me over these immensely testing ice falls. I became suddenly and completely at one with ice and snow, and able to meet and flow into it.

A new sensation. I became a snowflake, an icicle; and all the carefree joy of living which these elements possess became mine. Each step was a progress in sensing new ways of loving and entering into the outer skin of our great earth body. I became quite unconscious of Joe or anyone around me, excepting the varied layers of etheric beings and nature spirits.

181

As we rose, I saw these spirits rising to great vibratory power, until I began to see and hear the great communions of the peaks, the harmony within the discord of this immense instrument for conducting, duplicating, preserving, storing, and eventually dispensing the God-consciousness among men. It was so awesome in its grandeur – the communion between the Great Spirits and the Almighty – that I felt an unworthy eavesdropper, suddenly thrown into the centre of this vast expanse of Godfulness. I felt ashamed of my ability to hear, and my inability to grasp, and I longed with all my being for light to enter my mind, and an interpreter to come to my aid; and immediately there beside me stood a radiant figure. Joe has described this to you, but I, unable still to accept marvels in the way of the old, I questioned, 'Why am I here and unable to reach and absorb this marvellous wisdom?' And over the glittering expanse of light, came a voice unlike anything I have ever heard before, telling me to be still and know. The figure of Light came close to me, and I began to feel the power to become absorbed by the outer tentacles of this radiating presence – I saw and understood. But no words can frame the sense of utter holiness which enveloped me. It was beyond my power to hold it for long, but what I held I knew would be mine from that moment to eternity.

Hugh

# Part VII

*Sally's last letter.*
*Envoi*

*During a recent visit to Cynthia, I wrote (as I always do) to my daughter Sally, suggesting that she should describe to me her present life – her actual awareness now, compared with her first waking after physical death; her work, interests, recreations: in brief, that she should write an autobiographical sketch of her sixteen years in 'the Beyond'. What follows is her reply, written through Cynthia. R.L.*

Mummy, what an exercise you have set me! I will do my very best, but you know, I have been on other planes of vibration and colour and sound for which you have no words. These experiences are outside time and space and individuality, where we lose our personal consciousness altogether, knowing that it is only a temporary exercise – that we have to return to our job in our own personality. But for a space of, shall I call it 'time' for lack of another word, we are able to sink into the Great Consciousness. This is something so superb that it is beyond all explaining; you just have to experience it. But I will try to work up to this point so far as I can.

On coming over with no knowledge or understanding I had to begin at the beginning; all that you know. Then Pat came into my life and I rose from the crowd of 'don't knows' into the mass of lovely outflowing people who 'know', and I began to live again in a vital way. Now that sounds as though the 'don't knows' were left to themselves; they are, because they go on wishing it so deeply, hugging their old grievances and going on being miserable and lonely to such an extent that no one can penetrate and if they do, the 'don't knows' brush them aside and go on grumbling. But the moment light begins to dawn they are off like me, into a world of light and colour and music.

I drifted about in this wonder-world for a long time. No one urges you to move on until you have completely saturated yourself with the vibs you hunger for; and then when I began looking round Pat came to me and said: 'How about a journey?'

'Where to?' I asked.

'The question is, shall it be on this plane, the next plane, or the earth plane, to see if you can understand how they all merge together?'

185

I said: 'The earth plane; I want to know how I write through Cynthia, and why she can hear me.'

So we came back to the coarse vibs of earth, but they had changed, and I began to see both planes; I could see the two bodies in everything and everybody, and I was so excited. I saw your etheric body, Mummy, and Cynthia's, and I understood how sound of a peculiar sort penetrates without any physical vibs. I watched and listened and thought, and Pat took me into churches and on to mountains and down to the bottom of the sea; and here I began to use another set of vibs altogether: they are a mixture of astral, etheric and X vibs. Now it's the X-vibs that I found so enthralling, and I began to find them all over the place. At first I discovered them for myself on the ocean bed. They lay in a mass of scintillating colour, and I asked Pat what they were. She took up a handful and threw them into her aura, and urged me to do the same. At first I just felt rather giddy; then I began to move unconsciously, and I asked Pat what was happening.

'You are floating away into the next dimension or plane. Don't be frightened, I am coming too.'

So we found ourselves in another land of exquisite beauty. The scents of this plane were like the most wonderful garden you've ever known, and I began to sense the colour and scent all over me. My feet were sensing the same things independently. Now this kind of 3D, 4D, 5D, 6D consciousness was very disturbing at first. It's so much easier to smell only with your nose, and not with your ears and toes and everything else thrown in. I gasped at the enlarged awareness of my body, and felt quite staggered by it.

Pat stood by explaining and calming me, or I should have become absolutely bonkers; but I did not, and after a time I began to orientate myself and enjoyed this tremendous enlargement. I asked Pat if I could rest for a time before going further and she agreed. I became so excited by this awareness that I couldn't think of anything else. Pat seeing my obsession reminded me that we can't go ahead without doing something to help those less fortunate; so before I knew what had happened I was back in a hospital ward among the healers trying to help the children who were leaving their bodies, and beginning the very first stage of their etheric journey.

I have so enjoyed writing that because it clears my head and puts the sequence of the growth of awareness in its right place.

*　　　*　　　*

Oh, Mummy, here we are again – now it become more difficult. I had gained the awareness of my whole body, and of course this took time and a lot of practice, but it was in this state that I was allowed to leave earth and penetrate the stratosphere. I stayed there for a long time. When I say stratosphere, I mean the etheric and astral part as well as the material part; I became quite aligned with the vibs in this strange country of the air.

I began to live as though at sea, without grass or trees or flowers, and instead of the actual plant life which I adore, I was among the vibs which go towards the creation of this wonderful multiple vegetable kingdom. And in this forcing house there exist all the tiny entities which deal with early growth. They are of all shapes and sizes; they are like little drops of love, each one caring and giving the life essence of love to every embryo seedling before it becomes airborne towards earth. On a further belt of this life-and-love-giving area I came upon the embryo birds and animals and fishes; and last of all I came upon embryo *man*. The seeds of baby life were all packed away with the divine essences of this sphere. All life appertaining to earth was created and fostered within this belt of all-knowing Divinity.

Of course this was far beyond my capacity to accept; or to understand all the magnificent facets of this amazing vibration. I looked and listened and wandered endlessly in these strange places, where life begins, or seems to begin; and when I had gathered all I could contain within my limited understanding, Pat said: 'Now I am going to show you the world of minerals. They have their birth in the planets, and far away in distant stars.'

I said, 'This seems strange to me, I thought minerals were the

187

creation of earth.' But no, they, above all entities, have the durability for distant travel, and upon those tiny pinprick lights from a thousand thousand stars our minerals were born. The first seeds were born in the nebulae, and they acted like magnets as the nebulae gradually solidified and the tiny seeds within germinated to become a magnetic field, and called to their brother and sister minerals in the distant spheres to grow and replenish them. And so the earth formed itself from the outside help of countless tiny rays borne through space.

I had to see and learn and accept all this teaching, but not all at once. It was only sometimes given to me, when I was able to see and follow the rays into the very heart of earth. It was given to me between spells of ordinary working for those who were less advanced, like the children in the hospital ward I told you about.

I became aware of all this through my entire body; when entering the earth one uses the whole of one's awareness to the last degree. I became very fond of earth, it was so homely and welcoming, and such a change from the stratosphere which had such immense spaces that even to us in advanced stages of awareness it seems rather bleak. Here, wrapped within the strata of earth I felt myself back in the stage of metal formation. I became coal and iron; I saw and felt all the memories of growth that they held within their grasp; the sunlit forests, the peat bogs, finally the black coal glistening round me: all this had to become mine. I had to live within the consciousness of every different living thing, moving down through animals and fishes to the very rocks beneath my feet. Each had a whole book of memories awaiting my intake brain; and once we accept a truth here, it remains; there is no forgetting on these planes or in these bodies.

And so we venture on through space, becoming more and more a part of the universal essence from which all things are fashioned; and with each step of awareness we gain life and yet more life, we become more vital and able to match ourselves in vibratory strength to the great central heart of *all-living*.

My love,<br>Sally

# ENVOI

*From the great Spirits who guard Iona*

We want to instil into you the power to move by your own volition. By that I mean over the surface of the earth using the currents to empower your legs; you must conform to the rhythm of earth. Try feeling a force that impels you. Call upon it and do not hurry. Take the power as though it were speeding you down hill. This is easy on Iona. Try it. Ask the earth to help you, ask the rocks to float you off the surface – recognize levitation.

You are at one with gravitation, you can use it in different ways. Where are your links with the birds? They defy gravitation as a pull downwards. Draw the forces of air into your being. You ask for the great source of power, but you do not specialize. You have here on Iona a unique chance to make links with the creatures of air. I do not limit them to birds but to all forces, currents and entities which move by their own volition. You can become allied to them. Ask, and it will be granted unto you.

Man thinks only of himself, but he is only one among the many chains of life that encircle our earthly creation. To each will come an awakening – a moment of vision. Then you will find the trees, the birds, the fishes will converse with you as easily as they do with us. Nor do the waters, rivers, or clouds remain dumb.

All things within your sight, hearing and feeling are due to register expectant life.

When you have learnt to reach out to the lifting rays and discarded the surface of the earth, when you are in the air powered by your own volition – then you will begin to enter THE KINGDOM.